The Gray Book

By Sons of Confederate Veterans

Published by Pantianos Classics

ISBN-13: 9781981419364

First published in 1920

Contents

Introduction iv

The Generally Misunderstood Emancipation Proclamation 10

The South Not Responsible for Slavery 21

Treatment of Prisoners in the Confederacy ... 34

The South in the Matter of Pensions 64

Injustice to the South 70

The Secession of 1861 Founded Upon Legal Right 81

The South and Germany 100

Officers 106

Introduction

THE reasons for the Gray Book are purely defensive and on behalf of the truth of history, and the call for this publication comes from attacks, past, present and continuing, upon the history, people and institutions of this Southern section of our united country.

These attacks and untruthful presentations of so-called history demand refutation, for the South cannot surrender its birthright and we pray the day may never dawn when it will be willing to abandon the truth in a cowardly or sluggish spirit of pacifism. Nor do we care to see the day come when

"The lie, its work well done, shall rot,
Truth is strong and will prevail,
When none shall care if it prevail or not."

During the Great War, when the South and all other parts of our country were straining every nerve to defeat a common foe, strange and unbelievable as it may seem at such a time of crisis, there was a most remarkable flood of misrepresentation, false analogy, and distorted historical statements concerning our American history as it particularly relates to the Southern people. Ignorance, as well as deliberate distortion of facts, contributed to this unfortunate and ill-timed display.

A distinguished New Englander writing to a prominent officer of the Sons of Confederate Veterans, stated, "so far as New England is concerned, prejudice is still deep," and those who keep abreast of things know that this state of affairs is not confined to that section. We have the deliberate statement of a well-known writer and literary worker, who knows whereof he speaks, that "much atrocious sectionalism" tries to get into "publications which will have a very wide circulation in a patriotic capacity."

Innumerable examples are on file and could be quoted but no one who reads at all could have failed to note this mass of unfair and untruthful statements which for years has filled newspapers, magazines and periodicals of the North.

Nor has this defamation ceased with the end of the Great War—it still goes on, unabated, and there is a constant and strong stream of misrepresentation and false historical statement flowing from the North. Moreover, this constant reiteration of misstatement and falsehood has had the effect of totally misleading and blinding to the truth of our country's history foreigners who would naturally be unbiased and neutral. This was abundantly proven by Lloyd George's remarkable cable to the New York Times on the occasion of Lincoln's birthday during the las year of the Great War, "we are fighting the same battle which your countrymen fought under Lincoln's leadership fifty years ago. Lincoln did not shrink from vindicating of the union and freedom by the terrible instrument of war."

It is scarcely necessary to call attention to the totally untrue inferences to be drawn from this utterance, addressed to the world at large by England's leading statesman. And in France when Leon Buorgeoise cited the trial and execution of Major Wirz as a legal precedent for the trial of the German Kaiser by the Allies, he exhibited the same total misconception of the truth of our history, misled of course by years of false Northern teaching of our country's affairs. And of late there has appeared a play, based upon the life of Abraham Lincoln, which has been witnessed by thousands of people in England and this country and tens of thousands of approving words written concerning it, which totally misrepresents the spirit of that time and whose whole trend is unfair and unjust to the South.

One of the points upon which the South is most frequently and pointedly assailed and misrepresented is the claim that the North fought the war to free the slaves. This statement is contrary to the assertions of Lincoln, Grant and Sherman and contrary to all the common sense evidence of the times. With scarcely one soldier in twenty in the Southern Armies owning even one slave and with thousands of Northern soldiers being slave owners, is it reasonable to assert that each went to war to right against his own interests? Is it not a repulsive thought that any mind could be so constituted as to believe that Robert E. Lee, Albert Sidney Johnson and Stonewall Jackson fought their immortal fight to hold some negroes in slavery! Nothing could be more unfair or untruthful than to represent the North as going into the War Between the States as upon some holy crusade to free the slaves from their Southern owners, to whom, it may be remarked in passing, in very large measure they had been sold by this same North—and the money not refunded!

And yet a prominent American author makes this assertion in an article he wrote at the request of the United States Committee on Public information, which article thus misrepresenting the South and hypocritically lauding the North was taken by this government Committee to France and scattered through her schools and among her children to teach them what "sort of people we Americans are." Further, a well-known writer and former divine, wrote an article, using most offensive terms, misrepresenting the South, which was most prominently featured in the official publication of the Y. M. C. A., and was scattered through the cantonments and camps of France and this country during the war.

Instances without number could be quoted, but these few sample cases show the direction and nature of the tide of falsehood and misrepresentation constantly pouring upon the Southern people.

Another point upon which we are constantly misrepresented is the application of the term "rebellion" to the secession of the Southern states from the Union. Without going into details, it is a conceded fact that during the earlier days of the Union the right of a state to secede was generally recognized. This right was asserted more than once by states in the North, who later refused to allow the South to assert the same claim. Massachusetts was a prominent believer in the rights of secession in the early days. John Quincy Adams declared on the floor of Congress, at the time of the admission of Texas as a state, that New England ought to secede, while the Hartford Convention threatened similar steps while our country was actively engaged in the war of 1812. Even at the time when the North declared the South had no right to secede, although having themselves asserted that right previously, we see West Virginia encouraged and assisted in secession from the mother state, while of late years the secession of Panama from Colombia was not only recognized by this government, but the forces of the United States made the secession an accomplished fact. The South is willing to stand by her record as to secession—she is unwilling to submit to the false claims now asserted by the North that the war was waged to grant liberty to suffering slaves.

In the face of this state of affairs, the Sons of Confederate Veterans have determined to offer refutation of a part at least of the false history which almost overwhelms us and through this issue of this modest book, which we now offer, we hope to attract attention to the truth, and do, in our feeble way, our part toward establishing it.

A. H. Jennings, Chairman.

The Gray Book Committee S. C. V.
Arthur H. Jennings, Chairman,
Lynchburg, Va.
Matthew Page Andrews,
Baltimore, Md.
C. H. Fauntleroy,
St. Louis, Mo.

The Generally Misunderstood Emancipation Proclamation

THERE is no document so little read or so widely misunderstood as the Emancipation Proclamation—there is no subject so entirely misstated as Lincoln's connection with, and attitude toward, freeing the negro.

Lincoln, who never freed a slave, is called "The Emancipator" while The Emancipation Proclamation, a war measure of the sternest description, holding within its possibilities an untold measure of woe for the South, is almost universally hailed as a great "humanitarian" document!

To those who wish to know the truth, attention is directed to these several points especially—the document is self-styled "a war measure; it not only did not free a single slave (this was done long afterward by Congressional action and the 13th amendment) but it expressly and particularly continued to hold in bondage the only slaves it could have freed, viz., those in country held by Federal armies and under the jurisdiction of the United States government; intended as a war measure to demoralize the South and destroy the morale of Southern armies there is a pointed hint at servile insurrection in paragraph third from the last in the proclamation of January 1st, 1863.

Attention is also called to Lincoln's attitude toward freeing the negro, as clearly expressed by him in a letter to Horace Greely, just prior to issuing the proclamation.

This letter, inserted below, is copied faithfully from the files of the New York Tribune now in the Congressional Library. It most abundantly speaks for itself. In it Lincoln makes use of expressions which entirely dispose of any claim that he was waging war to free the slaves and which confound those who so persistently misrepresent the causes of the war between the states.

"My paramount object," he says, "in this struggle is to save the Union, and is not, either to save or destroy slavery. If I could save the Union without freeing any slave I would do it; and if I could save it by freeing all the slaves, I would do it. What I do about slavery and the colored race I do because I believe it helps to save the Union."

This letter and the terms and restrictions of the Proclamation itself show beyond any doubt the entirely warlike purpose of the proclamation and the entire absence of any humanitarian element either in Lincoln's purposes in promulgating it or in the provisions of the instrument itself.

Lincoln's Letter to Greeley, (from Vol. 22 New York Tribune, August 25, 1862, page 4, column 3, on file in Congressional Library), with a few preliminary and nonessential sentences omitted:

Executive Mansion, Washington,
August 22, 1862.
"Hon. Horace Greeley:

Dear Sir:

I would save the Union. I would save it the shortest way under the constitution. The sooner the National authority can be restored, the nearer the Union will be 'the Union as it was. 7 If there be those who would not save the Union unless they could at the same time save slavery, I do not agree with them. My paramount to those who would not save the Union unless they could at the same V time destroy slavery, I do not agree with them. My paramount object in this struggle is to save the Union, and is not either to save or destroy slavery. If I could save the Union without freeing any slave, I would do it; and if I could save it by freeing all the slaves, I would do it; and if I could save it by freeing some and leaving others alone, I would also do that. What I do about slavery and the colored race, I do because I believe it helps to save this Union; and what I forbear, I forbear because I do not believe it would help to save the Union. I have here stated my purpose according to my view of official duty and I intend no modification of my oft expressed personal wish that all men, everywhere, could be free.

Yours,
A. Lincoln."

Here follows the preliminary proclamation of Sept. 22, 1862, and then afterward the "Emancipation Proclamation" itself, exempting from its provisions all those slaves in territory held by Federal arms and under jurisdiction of he U. S. government.

By the President of the United States of America

A Proclamation

I, Abraham Lincoln, President of the United States of America, and Commander-in-Chief of the Army and Navy thereof, do hereby proclaim and declare that hereafter, as heretofore, the war will be prosecuted for the object of practically restoring the constitutional relation between the United States and each of the States and the people thereof in which States that relation is or may be suspended or distributed.

That it is my purpose, upon the next meeting of Congress, to again recommend the adoption of a practical measure tendering pecuniary aid to the free acceptance or rejection of all slave States, so called, the people whereof may not then be in rebellion against the United States, and which States may then have voluntarily adopted, or thereafter may voluntarily adopt, immediate or gradual abolishment of slavery within their respective limits; and that the effort to colonize persons of African descent with their consent upon this continent or elsewhere, with the previously obtained consent of the governments existing there, will he continued.

That on the 1st day of January, A.D. 1863 all persons held as slaves within any State or designated part of a State the people whereof shall then be in rebellion against the United States shall be then, thenceforward, and forever free; and the executive government of the United States, including the military and naval authority thereof, will recognize and maintain the freedom of such persons and will do no act or acts to repress such persons, or any of them, in any efforts they may make for their actual freedom.

That the Executive will on the 1st day of January aforesaid, by proclamation, designate the States and parts of States, if any, in which the people thereof, respectively, shall then be in rebellion against the United States; and the fact that any State or the people thereof shall on that day be in good faith represented in the Congress of the United States by members chosen thereto at elections wherein a majority of the qualified voters of such State shall have participated shall, in the absence of strong countervailing testimony, he deemed conclusive evidence that such State and the people thereof are not then in rebellion against the United States.

That attention is hereby called to an act of Congress entitled "An act to make an additional article of war" approved March 13, 1862, and which act is in the words and figure following:

"Be it enacted by the Senate and House of Representatives of the United States of America in Congress assembled, That hereafter the following shall be promulgated as an additional article of war for the government of the Army of the United States, and shall be obeyed and observed as such:

Art.—All officers or persons in the military or naval service of the United States are prohibited from employing any of the forces under their respective commands for the purpose of returning fugitives from service or labor who may have escaped from any persons to whom such service or labor is claimed to be due, and any officer who should be found guilty by a court-martial of violating this article shall be dismissed from the service.

Sec. 2. And be it further enacted, That this act shall take effect from and after its passage."

Also to the ninth and tenth sections of an act entitled "An act to suppress insurrection, to punish treason and rebellion, to seize and confiscate the property of rebels, and for other purposes," approved July 17 1862, and which sections are in the words and figures following:

Sec. 9. And be it further enacted, That all slaves of persons who shall hereafter be engaged in rebellion against the Government of the United States, or who shall in any way give aid or comfort thereto, escaping from such persons and taking refuge within the lines of the army, and all slaves captured from such persons or deserted by them and coming under the control of the Government of the United States, and all slaves of such persons found on (or) being within any place occupied by rebel forces and afterwards occupied by the forces of the United States, shall be deemed captives of war and shall be forever free of their servitude and not again held as slaves.

Sec. 10. And be it further enacted, That no slave escaping into any State, Territory, or the District of Columbia from any other State shall be delivered up or in any way impeded or hindered of his liberty except for crime or some offense against the laws, unless the person claiming said fugitive shall first make oath that the person to whom the labor or service of such fugitive is alleged to be due is his lawful owner and has not borne arms against the United States in the present rebellion nor in any way given aid and comfort thereto; and no person engaged in the military or naval service of the United States shall, under any pretense whatever, assume to decide on the validity of the claim of any person to the service or labor of any other person or surrender up any such person to the claimant on pain of being dismissed from the service."

And I do hereby enjoin upon and order all persons engaged in the military and naval service of the United States to observe, obey, and enforce within their respective spheres of service the act and sections above recited.

And the Executive will in due time recommend that all citizens of the United States who shall have remained loyal thereto throughout the rebellion shall, upon the restoration of the constitutional relation between the

United States and their respective States and people, if that relation shall have been suspended or disturbed, be compensated for all losses by acts of the United States, including the loss of slaves.

In witness whereof I have hereunto set my hand and caused the seal of the United States to be affixed.

Done at the City of Washington, this 22d day of September, A. D. 1862, and of the Independence of the United States the eighty-seventh.

Abraham Lincoln.

By the President:
William H. Seward, *Secretary of State.*

Taken from "A Compilation of the Messages and Papers of the- Presidents 1789-1897, published by authority of Congress by James D. Richardson, a Representative from the State of Tennessee, Volume VI, Page 96."

By the President of the United States of America

A Proclamation

Whereas on the 22d day of September, A. D. 1862, a proclamation was issued by the President of the United States, containing, among other things, the following, to wit:

"That on the 1st day of January, A. I). 1868, all persons held as slaves within any State or designated part of a State the people whereof shall then be in rebellion against the United States shall be then, thenceforward, and forever free; and the executive government of the United States, including the military and naval authority thereof, will recognize and maintain the freedom of such persons and will do no act or acts to repress such persons, or any of them, in any efforts they may make for their actual freedom.

That the Executive will on the 1st day of January aforesaid, by proclamation, designated the States and parts of States, if any, in which the people thereof, respectively, shall then be in rebellion against the United States ; and the fact that any State or the people thereof shall on that day be in good faith represented in the Congress of the United States by members chosen thereto at elections wherein a majority of the qualified voters of such States shall have participated shall, in the absence of strong countervailing testimony, be deemed conclusive evidence that such State and the people thereof are not then in rebellion against the United States."

Now, therefore, I, Abraham Lincoln, President of the United States, by virtue of the power in me vested as Commander-in-Chief of the Army and Navy of the United States in time of actual armed rebellion against the authority and Government of the United States, and as a fit and necessary war measure for suppressing said rebellion, do, on this 1st day of January, A. D. 1863, and in accordance with my purpose so to do, publicly proclaimed for the full period of one hundred days from the day first above mentioned, order and designate as the States and parts of States wherein the people thereof, respectively, are this day in rebellion against the United States the following, to wit:

Arkansas, Texas, Louisiana (except the parishes of St. Bernard, Plaquemines, Jefferson, St. John, St, Charles, St. James, Ascension, Assumption, Terrebonne, Lafourche, St. Mary, St. Martin, and Orleans, including the city of New Orleans), Mississippi, Alabama, Florida, Georgia, South Carolina, North Carolina, and Virginia (except the forty-eight counties designated as West Virginia, and also the counties of Berkeley, Accomac, Northampton, Elizabeth City, York, Princess Anne, and Norfolk, including the cities of Norfolk and Portsmouth), and which excepted parts are for the present left precisely as if this proclamation were not issued.

And by virtue of the power and for the purpose aforesaid, I do order and declare that all persons held as slaves within said designated States and parts of States are and henceforward shall be free, and that the executive government of the United States, including the military and naval authorities thereof, will recognize and maintain the freedom of said persons.

And I hereby enjoin upon the people so declared to be free to abstain from all violence, unless in necessary self-defense; and I recommend to them that in all cases when allowed they labor faithfully for reasonable wages.

And I further declare and make known that such persons of suitable condition will be received into the armed service of the United States to garrison forts, positions, stations, and other places and to man vessels of all sorts in said service.

And upon this act, sincerely believed to be an act of justice, warranted by the Constitution upon military necessity, I invoke the considerate judgment of mankind and the gracious favor of Almighty God.

In witness whereof I have hereunto set my hand and caused the seal of the United States to be affixed. Done at the city of Washington, this 1st day of January, A. D. 1863, and of the Independence of the United States of America the eighty-seventh.

Abraham Lincoln.

By the President:
William H. Seward, *Secretary of State.*

Taken from "A Compilation of the Messages and Papers of the Presidents 1789-1897, published by authority of Congress by James D. Richardson, a Representative from the State of Tennessee, Volume VI, Page 157."

The South Not Responsible for Slavery

Neither the introduction of Slaves into America nor their continued Importation can be Charged to the South. By Arthur II. Jennings, Chairman Gray Book Com.

Undoubtedly England, Spain and the Dutch were primarily and largely responsible for the introduction and the earlier importation of slaves to this country. As Bancroft says, "The sovereigns of England and Spain were the greatest slave merchants in the world."

Later on, this country came into prominence in the traffic in human bodies and DuBois, the negro historical writer says, "The American slave trade came to be carried on principally by United States capital, in United States ships, officered by United States citizens and under the United States flag." Supporting this, Dr. Phillips of Tulane University in his section of "The South in the Building of the Nation," states, "The great volume of the slave traffic from the earlier 17th century onward was carried on by English and Yankee vessels, with some competition from the French and the Dutch."

The responsibility for this home, or American, participation in the slave importing business rests primarily and principally upon New England and likewise, very largely, upon New York. It was a boast and a taunt of pre-war days with pro-slavery orators that, "The North imported slaves, the South only bought them"—and historians assert that "there is some truth in the assertion."

Indeed, it has been widely claimed that "No Southern man or Southern ship ever brought a slave to the United States," and while this statement is disputed and is perhaps not strictly true according to the letter, it is undoubtedly true in spirit, for the cases where a Southern man or Southern ship could be charged with importing slaves are few indeed, while New England, as well as New York, were openly and boldly engaged in the traffic, employing hundreds of ships in the nefarious business.

"Slavery," says Henry Watterson, in the Louisville Courier Journal, "existed in the beginning North and South. But the North finding slave labor unsuited to its needs and, therefore, unprofitable, sold its slaves to the South, not forgetting to pocket the money it got for them, *having indeed at great profit brought them over from Africa in its ships.*

Mr. Cecil Chesterman, a distinguished English historian, in his "History of the United States" says on this point, "The North had been the original slave traders. The African slave trade had been their particular industry. Boston itself had risen to prosperity on the profits of the abominable traffic."

The Marquis of Lothian, in his "Confederate Secession" makes the statement that "out of 1500 American slave traders, only five were from the South," but apparently this statement is contradicted later in his volume when he says, "out of 202 slavers entering the port of Charleston, S. C, in four years, 1796 to 1799 inclusive, 91 were English, 88 Yankees, 10 were French and 13 South. * * * "

Many indeed are the authorities that support the statement that the South did not import slaves. "Slavery/' says Senator John W. Daniel of Virginia," was thrust on the South, an uninvited, aye, a forbidden guest" and Dr. Charles Morris, in his "History of Civilization" says "The institution of slavery was not of their making; it had been thrust upon their fathers against their violent opposition."

Mrs. Sea, in her book, "The Synoptical Review of Slavery," says "'I have heard the statement made, and gentlemen of the highest standing for scholarly attainment given as authority, that no Southern man ever owned a slave ship and that no slave ship handled by a Southern man ever brought a cargo of slaves from Africa,"

Dr. Lyon G. Tyler, the scholarly President of William and Mary College, Virginia, and an authority, says, regarding this statement, "I am sure it can be said that no Southern man or Southern ship, as far as is known, engaged in the slave trade."

References to Southern ships or Southern men as engaged in the slave importing business are at best vague. The famous case of the "Wanderer," one of the most noted of slave trading vessels, is often mentioned and her ownership is credited to men of Charleston and Savannah, but even if this be true she was built in New York, her captain was a New York man, and a member of the New York Yacht Club and the "Wanderer" sailed under the proud flag of that Club when she went to the Congo after slaves. Her captain was later expelled from the club for this offense.

The fact that there was domestic traffic in slaves, some of this domestic traffic being carried on through coastwise trading, seems to have confused some and induced them to believe the South engaged in the slave importing business. On the other hand, the responsibility of New England and New York for the almost exclusive monopoly of domestic participation in the slave importing "business is most clearly established. Massachusetts looms largely to the front when investigation into this gruesome subject is pursued. The first slave ship of this country, the "Desire," was fitted out in Massachusetts, and set sail for the coast of Africa from Marblehead. Massachusetts was the first of all the colonies to authorize the establishment of slavery by statute law, doing this some decades before her example was followed by any of the Southern colonies. The first statute establishing slavery in America is embodied in the Code of the Massachusetts Colony in New England, adopted in 1641, and it should be realized that slave trading in Massachusetts was not a private enterprise but was carried on by authority of the Plymouth Rock colony.

The Puritans early evinced a tendency to enslave Indian captives and sell them out of the country, and from that early day down to a period practically after the War Between the States had begun (for the last slave ship, the Nightingale, sailing from Boston and fitted out there, with 900 slaves on board was captured at the mouth of the Congo River after the war had started) New England, with Massachusetts leading', stood preeminent in the slave trade.

Much of the prominence and wealth of these states was derived from the slave trade and the commercial importance of such towns as Newport, Rhode Island, was based entirely upon the traffic. Tt is stated that Faneuil Hall, the famous "Cradle of Liberty" where so many abolition speeches, denunciatory of the South were made, was built with money earned in the slave traffic, as Peter Faneuil was actively engaged in it. "It was a traffic," says Dr. Phillips, in 'The South in Building of the Nation,' "in which highly honorable men like Peter Faneuil engaged and which the Puritans did not condemn in the Colonial period." Stephen Girard is another prominent philanthropist of the North who made money in slaves, working large numbers of them on a Louisiana sugar plantation which he owned, and it is asserted that Girard College was built with money earned by the labors of these slaves.

In fact, DuBois asserts that the New England conscience which would not allow slavery to flourish on the sacred soil of Massachusetts did not hesitate to seize the profits resulting from the rape of slaves from their African homes and their sale to Southern planters. But, according to John Adams, it was not a tender conscience but an economic reason upon which the forbidding of slaves in Massachusetts was based, for he is quoted as saying, "Argument might have had some weight in the abolition of slavery in Massachusetts, but the real cause was the multiplication of laboring white people who no longer would surfer the rich to employ these sable rivals so much to their injury." Thomas Jefferson, who had introduced a scathing denunciation of, and protest against, the slave trade in the Declaration of Independence, withdrew it upon the insistence of Adams and other New Englanders, and he indulges in the following little bit of sarcasm at their expense, "our Northern friends who were tender under these censures, for, though their people have very few slaves, yet they had been considerable carriers of them to others."

Economic reasons were the base of abolition of slavery in New England. There is abundance of record to show dissatisfaction with negro labor, who were stated to be "eye servants, great thieves, much addicted to lying and stealing," and the superiority of white labor was brought prominently forward. Furthermore, the mortality of the negroes in the cold New England climate was great and figures were brought forward to show how their importation into the section was not "profitable." Governor Dudley in a formal report in 1708 stated "negroes have been found unprofitable investments, the planters preferring white servants."

Boston was all along prominent in the slave trade, the "Continental Monthly" of New York, as late as January, 1862, being quoted as saying, "The city of New York has been until late (1862) the principal port of the world for this infamous traffic, the cities of Portland and Boston being only second to her in that distinction." "Slave dealers," it continues, "added much to the wealth of our metropolis."

Vessels from Massachusetts, Rhode Island, Connecticut, and New Hampshire were early and largely engaged in the slave trade, and it is a very significant fact that while duties, more or less heavy, were imposed upon the imported slaves in Southern harbors, and other harbors of the country, the ports of New England were offered as a free exchange mart for slavers.

New England *citizens* were traders by instinct and profession, and with the birth of commerce in the New World they eagerly turned to the high profits of the African slave trade and made it a regular business. The "Hartford Courant" in an issue of July, 1916, said, "Northern rum had much to do with the extension of slavery in the South. Many people in this state (Connecticut) as well as in Boston, made snug fortunes for themselves by sending rum to Africa to be exchanged for slaves and then selling the slaves to the planters of Southern states."

Rhode Island at an early date had 150 vessels engaged in the slave trade, while at a later date, when New York had loomed to the front of the trade, the New York "Journal of Commerce" is quoted as saying, "Few of our readers are aware of the extent to which this infernal traffic is carried on by vessels clearing from New York and down town merchants of wealth and respectability are engaged extensively in buying and selling African negroes, and have been for an indefinite number of years."

As early as 1711 a slave market was established in New York City in the neighborhood of Wall street where slaves from Africa were brought to supply the Southern market. There was another prominent slave market in Boston. The slaves were hurried into the South as fast as possible as hundreds died from cold and exposure and the sudden change from a tropic African climate to a bleak Northern temperature. The United States Dept. Marshall for that New York district reported in 1856 that "the business of fitting out slavers was never prosecuted with greater energy than at present." In a year and a half preceding the War Between the States eighty-five slave trading vessels are reported as fitting out in New York harbor and DuBois writes that, "from 1850 to 1860 the fitting out of slavers became a flourishing business in the United States and centered in New York City."

Although Massachusetts and New York were thus prominent in the business of enslaving and importing Africans and selling them to South America and the Southern colonics, and later the Southern states in the Union, oilier parts of New England took most prominent part in the slave trade. Indeed, in the "Reminiscences of Samuel Hopkins," Rhode Island is said to have been "more deeply interested in the slave trade than any other colony in New England and has enslaved more Africans."

Thus beginning with that first slave ship of this country, the "Desire" of Marblehead, Mass., the slave trade flourished in New England and New York. The favorite method was to exchange rum for negroes and to sell the negroes to the Southern plantations. Federal laws were powerless to hold in check the keenness for this profitable traffic in human flesh. As late as 1850, the noted slave smuggler, Drake, who flourished and operated along the Gulf Coast, is reported to have said, "Slave trading is growing more profitable every year, and if you should hang all the Yankee merchants engaged in it, hundreds more would take their places."

The outlawing of the traffic seemed but to stimulate it. From the very inception of the institution of slavery in this country there was protest and action against it throughout the Southern colonies. The vigorous action of Virginia and her protests to the royal government to prohibit the further importation of slaves to her territory are well known. We have seen how Jefferson introduced into the Declaration of Independence a protest against the slave trade which he withdrew at the behest of New England. Every prominent man in Virginia at this period was in favor of gradual emancipation and there were more than five times as many members of abolition societies in the South than in the North. Only with the rise of the rabid abolitionists of New England and their fierce denunciations of the South did the South abandon hope of gradual emancipation. Touching this, Mr. Cecil Chesterman, quoted above, states very pointedly in his "History of the United States," "what could exceed the effrontery of men" asked the Southerner, "who reproach us with grave personal sin in owning property which they themselves sold us and the price of which is at this moment in their pockets?" Virginia legislated against slavery over a score of times; South Carolina, protested against it as early as 1727, and in Georgia there was absolute prohibition of it by law. Let it be remembered that when the National Government took action and the slavery prohibition laws of Congress went into effect in 1808, every Southern state had prohibited it.

But, as stated, the outlawing of the traffic seemed but to stimulate it. In the earlier years of the 19th century thousands of slaves were imported into this country. In the year 1819, Gen. James Talmadge, speaking in the House of Representatives, declared: "It is a well known fact that about 14,000 slaves have been brought into our country this year." And Sergeant, of Pennsylvania, said: "It is notorious that in spite of the utmost vigilance that can be employed, African negroes are clandestinely brought in and sold as slaves."

This "vigilance" he speaks of, however, was much ridiculed by others, and it was openly hinted that the efforts of the Federal authorities to suppress the trade, even the look-out for slavers along the African coast as conducted by vessels of the United States Navy, were merely perfunctory, Blake in his "History of Slavery and the Slave Trade," published in 1857, says: "It is stated upon good authority that in 1844 more slaves were carried away from Africa in ships than in 1744 when the trade was legal and in full vigor;" while in the year immediately preceding the opening of the War Between the States, John C. Underwood is quoted as writing to the New York Tribune: "I have ample evidence of the fact that the reopening of the African slave trade is an accomplished fact and the traffic is brisk." Not only was the traffic brisk with the United States but thousands of slaves were being smuggled into Brazil.

Southern members of Congress complained of the violations of the law and the illegal importation of slaves into their territory. Smith, of South Carolina, said on the floor of Congress in 1819: "Our Northern friends are not afraid to furnish the Southern States with Africans;" and in 1819, Middleton, of South Carolina, and Wright, of Virginia, estimated the illicit introduction of slaves at from 1300 to 1500 respectively.

There is interest in the striking fact that one year before the outbreak of the War Between the States, and at the time when the rabid abolitionists of New England and the North were most vigorous in their denunciations of the South and the slave holders, there were in Massachusetts only 9000 free negroes, while in Virginia there were 53,000 of these negroes, free, and able to go where they pleased; and it is significant that about as many free negroes chose to live in Southern slave holding states as dwelt in Northern states; and many of these free negroes owned slaves themselves and were well-to-do citizens. In the city of Charleston, S. C, some three hundred free negroes owned slaves themselves.

In closing this article the following letter, which appeared in the columns of the New Orleans Picayune years ago, may be of interest:

"My father, Capt. John Julius Guthrie, then of the United States Navy, while executive officer of the sloop of war "Saratoga" on April 21st, 1861, captured at the mouth of the Congo River, on the west coast of Africa, the slave ship 'Nightingale' with 900 slaves aboard. The slaver was owned, manned and equipped in the city of Boston, Mass., and in reference to the date it will appear that her capture was after the assault on Fort Sumter and the Baltimore riot consequent upon the passage of the 6th Massachusetts Regiment through the city. This was the last slaver captured by an American war ship and as my father soon after resigned and went in to the Confederate service, her captain and owners were never brought to trial. All this is a matter of record on file at the Navy Department in Washington. It will be seen that the last capture of a slaver was by a Southern officer and the good people of Massachusetts were engaged in this nefarious business at the beginning of our unhappy war."

(Signed) J. Julius Guthrie,

Portsmouth, Va.

Too Long has the South had the odium of slavery forced upon her. With the institution thrust upon her against her protest, the slaves flourished in her boundaries on account of climate, and economic conditions favored the spread of the institution itself. The facts set forth above indicate the innocence of the South in foisting this feature upon our national life, as well as her freedom from guilt in the continued importation of slaves into this country. While no claim is made for special virtue in that the South did not engage in the slave importing business as the North did, yet the facts as they exist are to her credit. With the facts in her favor, the South sits still under the false indictments constantly made against her by the section of our country most responsible for the whole trouble. Willing to abide by the verdict of posterity, if the verdict is based upon the truth, and not upon the false statements of Northern historians, writers and speakers, and willing to accept her share, her full share of due responsibility, this section, in justice to her dead who died gloriously in a maligned cause, and to her unborn children, inheritors of a glorious heritage, must set forth to the world the facts as they are, neither tainted with injustice to others nor burdened with hypocritical claims of righteousness for herself; and these facts will establish her in the proud position to which she has all along been entitled among the people of the earth.

Treatment of Prisoners in the Confederacy

By Matthew Page Andrews
Author of History of the United States, Dixie Book of Days, &c, &c.

Only a generation ago, Raphael Semmes, commander of the Confederate warship Alabama, was widely advertised as a "pirate" and Robert E. Lee was stigmatized as a "traitor." Thousands of young Americans were taught so to regard these Southern leaders. Now, however, these terms are nearly obsolete; while many Northern historians, such as Charles Francis Adams, who fought on the Federal side in the War of Secession, and Gamaliel Bradford, who grew up after the war, have delighted in honoring Lee and other Southern leaders as Americans whose character and achievements are the ennobling heritage of a united Nation.

It was more or less natural that Americans should have been led astray of the truth in the heat of sectional strife and partisan expression. Misconceptions have arisen out of every war. In fifty years, however, Americans have made greater progress in overcoming war prejudices than the people of other lands in twice or thrice that period.

This is encouraging, yet the fact that the greater number of our textbooks, and consequently our schools, teach that "the cause for which the South fought was unworthy ;" that the Southern leaders "were laboring under some of the most curious hallucinations which a student of history meets in the whole course of his researches;" and that "the South was the champion of the detested institution of slavery," indicates a lamentable state of historical ignorance on the part of those who should know better. The characters of the Southern leaders are no longer aspersed but their *motives are besmirched or clouded* and their cause unjustly condemned because it is still widely misunderstood. [1]

Furthermore, since the beginning of the World War of 1914, the conduct of the Prussians, together with the character of their cause, has been compared with the character of the Confederate conduct of the War of Secession, together with the cause and character of Southern statesmen. Reputable magazines of wide circulation and writers of prominence have compared Confederate treatment of prisoners with Prussian outrages in Belgium and France. American newspapers also have printed literally thousands of such comparative references. Fortunately, nine-tenths of these comparisons have been made through ignorance of the facts and not through any malicious desire of the authors to defame the fair name of a single fellow-American on the Confederate side or the "lost cause" which he represented with unsurpassed devotion and valor.

Side by side with these accusations, in some cases, generous praise is bestowed upon the former "pirate" Semmes as having furnished a model for warfare on the high seas; and it is freely stated that his observance of all the requirements of international custom arm of the dictates of humanity in civilized warfare held not only to the letter, but also to the full spirit of the law. It is not denied, also, that Lee, the Confederate chieftain and quondam "traitor" has offered the world the noblest example of orders of conduct for an army in the enemy's country that all history can show, and that these orders were also carried out "even to the protection of a farmer's fence rails!" The Boston Transcript, for example, took occasion, in 1917, to publish these orders in full.

Nevertheless, in regard to the treatment of prisoners, the sweeping condemnation of James G. Blaine, delivered in an outburst of war-inspired and partisan condemnation of the South is still, in a general way, believed by Americans who have, of late, been echoing them, although in milder terms and in *limitation of the number of those held to have been guilty.* Mr. Blaine declared some ten years after the war: "Mr. Davis [President of the Confederate States] was the author, knowingly, deliberately, guiltily, and willfully, of the gigantic murder and crime at Andersonville. And I here, *before God measuring my words, knowing their full extent and import* declare that neither the deeds of the Duke of Alva in the low countries, nor the massacre of Saint Bartholomew, nor the thumb screws and engines of torture of the Spanish Inquisition, begin to compare in atrocity with the hideous crimes of Andersonville."

Historians do not now accept this statement as true, solemnly made as it was by a man who, a few years later, barely missed election to the highest office in the gift of the people of the United States. Furthermore, American historians, even if inclined to bias, do not now go into any detail in the matter of these charges. They refer the reader, however, to a mass of matter the major part of which is as false today as when James G. Blaine based upon it his colossal libel of Jefferson Davis and the military and civil authorities of the Southern Confederacy. As above stated, the so-called "general" historian has dropped this matter in detail, though Mr. Blaine exclaimed dramatically that it would remain as the "blackest page" recorded in the annals of all time. [2] On the other hand, innumerable monographs have been written upon this subject, four-fifths of which are either false per se, or else based on false evidence such as that which has misled so many Americans, from the time of James G. Blaine and contemporary historians, to editors of and writers in magazines and newspapers of the second decade in the twentieth century. With this one notable exception, American history is rapidly freeing its narrative of misconception in all of its phases. It is here that we now find the last great stronghold of sectional misconception.

If four-fifths of the monographs on prison life in the South are false per se, or based on false evidence, it follows that one-fifth are true or approximately so. The writer has had the privilege of knowing personally a distinguished Union Veteran who suffered privations and hardships at Lib by Prison. Published in 1912, his story, as it affects his personal experiences, is doubtless true in every respect; yet this same good American helped to publish simultaneously another volume by one of his comrades that is a tissue of falsehood and slander from beginning to end. The veracious author seemed to take his mendacious comrade at his face value, and he advertised as worthy history a gross historical libel. [3]

Again with reference to a portion of the truthful fifth part of the testimony in monographs or special articles, it should be said that a concerted attempt has apparently been made by certain interested individuals and groups to cry down, suppress, or defame the authors of these monographs. The average good American citizen, who likes to believe that the people of one section "about average rip to" the people of another, is moved to amazement at the extreme violence of the attacks made upon men who, on this one subject, would say even the least in defense of their former opponents. "God knows we suffered there," said one of the ex-prisoners of Andersonville, "bill who found out that the Confederate soldier had our Pare and often less, and he was often as shoeless as we, in time, became. We were the worse oil' chiefly because of enforced confinement, hope deferred, and Longing for borne and freedom." Men who have made such statements as these or who have defended their former captors and fellow-countrymen Prom the charge of deliberate cruelty, have been bitterly attacked in Grand Army Posts—not by men of similar liberal ideals, but by narrow-minded men who were otherwise good citizens and by bounty-jumpers and deserters who made it their business to fan the flames of sectional passion so that the public would continue to support them in the way which has been exposed by Charles Francis Adams. In some eases, the thought of all this false testimony weighed like a heavy load upon the eon-sciences of patriotic Union Veterans who loved their whole country and honored their former Confederate foes as opponents worthy of their steel. One of these men who was thus moved to write what he held to be true had long looked forward to the honor of commanding his Department of the Grand Army of the Republic. His published narrative defending the motives of his former captors cost him this honor, even though it contained no single word or phrase that reflected unfavorably upon the cause of the North. An historian who undertook to inquire about the veracity of the narrative was told by well-meaning men across the Continent from the author that "the book was untrustworthy" and that the author was unreliable. A quiet and careful investigation was, however, made by him into the character and career of the "witness," and the favorable testimony of those in a position to know him best in all his relations led the historian to place the greatest confidence in his testimony. [4]

The charges preferred against the authorities of the Confederacy were, for several years, made the most important subject under consideration by the people and even the government of the United States. During that period, the magnitude and violence of the accusations obscured much more weighty and serious problems and placed the South on the defensive, because it was not the better element in the North but the radical and partisan minority that had, for the moment, the ear of the country and the world. Secretary Stanton used the following language in one of the official reports of the Federal Government: "*The enormity of the crime committed by the Rebels* towards our prisoners for the last several months is not known or realized by our people, and cannot but fill with horror the civilized world when the facts are fully revealed. There appears to have been *a deliberate system of savage and barbarous treatment and starvation*, the result of which will be that few, (if any) of the prisoners that have been in their hands during the past winter will ever again be in a condition to render any service, or even to enjoy life." At the same time, the United States Sanitary Commission declared that: "The evidence *proves, beyond all manner of doubt, a determination on the part of the Rebel authorities, deliberately and, persistently practiced* for a long time past, to subject those of our soldiers who have been so unfortunate as to fall into their hands to a system of treatment which has resulted in reducing many of those who have survived and been permitted to return to us to a condition, both physically and mentally, which no language we can use can adequately describe

The conclusion is unavoidable, therefore, that these privations and sufferings *have been designedly inflicted by the military and other authorities of the Rebel Government, and could not have been due to causes which such authorities could not control."*

A widely circulated volume by a former prisoner at Andersonville, the largest of the Confederate prison camps, contains the following statement: "Inside of this inclosure, thirteen thousand, two hundred and fifty-three Union soldiers perished. There is no spot on the face of the earth where man's inhumanity to man was more fully demonstrated than in this terrible place, and the name of Andersonville will be a dark spot on American civilization for centuries to come. ... To Jefferson Davis, his cabinet advisers, and to the demons whom they sent to these prisons to carry out their devilish plans, and who appear to have been well adapted for that kind of work, belongs the infamy of perpetrating one of the most horrible crimes known in the history of the world, and one which will forever remain a blot and a stigma on that page of our country's history... And in all the Southern prisons, as near as could be ascertained, about 65,000 men fell victims to rebel barbarity. Who can doubt but that it was a fairly concocted scheme of their captors to destroy them, and that, too, in the most horrible manner."

The official Report of the Committee in Congress on the conduct of the war contains the following statement:

"The subsequent history of Andersonville has startled and shocked the world with a tale of horror, of woe, and death before unheard and unknown to civilization. No pen can describe, no painter sketch, no imagination comprehends its fearful and unutterable iniquity. It would seem that the concentrated madness of earth and hell had found its final Lodgement *in the breasts of those who inaugurated the Rebellion and controlled the policy the Confederate government, and that the prison at Andersonville had been selected* for the most, terrible human sacrifice which the world had ever seen. Into its narrow walls were crowded thirty-five thousand men, many of them the bravest and host, the most devoted and heroic of those grand armies which carried the flag of their country to final victory. For long and weary months here they suffered, maddened, were murdered and died . . . these men, these heroes, born in the Image of God, thus crouching and writhing in their terrible torture and calculating barbarity, stand forth in history as a monument of the surpassing horrors of Andersonville as it shall be seen and read in all future time, realizing in the studied torments of their prison house the ideal of Dante's Inferno and Milton's Hell."

Those historians who have at all investigated the matter regard such statements as partisan and untrue; but many historical writers who have not so investigated perpetuate in modified form, these same falsehoods. When, for instance, so great a periodical as Collier's Weekly descends to such sectionalism, it does so in ignorance and not in malice. For this reason, perhaps, any such injustice as the following is more to be deplored. In its issue of February 17, 1917, the leading editorial article is entitled "The Morals of Slavery" in which a resume is given of Prussian outrages in Belgium under Von Bissing. The writer, who may have been an occasional contributor of national and international prominence, draws the following comparison, italics inserted:

"The only prototype that the history of our own country affords for General Von Bissing is Captain Henry Wirz, commanding officer of Andersonville prison. He *pleaded 'military and economic necessity' as an excuse for his acts,* and in a general way defended his cruelties with the same arguments that have been advanced by the German Government in defending the invasion of Belgium, the shooting of hostages, and the merciless exploitation of the labor and resources of the country. *He acted under orders;* he did only what conditions compelled him to do. *His defense was supremely logical to minds that had grown tolerant of the harshness of war.* But even at a time when leniency was exercised in the treatment of spies, blockade runners, privateersmen, and freebooters, the Union Government drew the line at Wirz's offenses. The severe logician was tried in 1865 by a military commission and promptly hanged. It is to his credit that he did not attempt to justify his cruelty to the prisoners by pleading his intention of improving their morals."

Collier's Weekly is, perhaps, the most popular of the publications that reprinted, with variations, an ancient error. The history of the historical statement of the prison charges runs from the early "conviction of direct complicity" on the part of all the *civil and military authorities* of the Confederacy to the indirect charge against them through Captain Wirz, a poor subordinate of Swiss birth, who was one of the commandants at the Andersonville prison. Him his accusers hanged after the most unjust trial that this country has ever known. As late as 1917, the distinguished editor of "American State Trials" and the Vice-President of the International Law Association was so far led astray by the "evidence" as to prepare a preface to the volume, *which was separately printed and circulated,* approving the charges brought against Wirz as properly substantiated. [5]

It is recognized by all who have carefully investigated the prison question that the civil and military Committees and Commissions appointed under strongly partisan auspices to look into the prison question rendered reports that are now known to be false. Shortly afterwards, Southern officials, hampered as they were at that time, made replies to these accusations and published some of them. These replies of the Southern officials contend:

(1) That although it is not denied that there was terrible suffering and great mortality in Confederate prisons, this was due to circumstances beyond their control.

(2) That if the death rate be adduced as "circumstantial evidence of barbarity," the rate was as high or even higher in the majority of the prisons in the North, where there was an abundance of food and where shelter could easily be provided. [6]

(3) That in the South the same rations were given the prisoners and the guards; hut that variety in food could not be had or transported on the broken-down railway system of a non-manufacturing country, which system could not or did not provide sufficient clothes and food even for the Con federate soldiers in the field. [7]

(4) That the Confederacy had arranged for the exchange of prisoners by a special cartel, which cartel was deliberately disregarded by the Federal authorities. [8]

(5) That they offered to permit Federal Surgeons to bring medical supplies to the prisoners, which offer was not accepted.

(6) That, as the needs of the prisoners increased, they offered to buy (finally with cotton or with gold) supplies for the prisoners, which offer was ignored.

(7) That medicines had been treated by the Federal Government as contraband of war, so that the people of the South were often deprived of necessary remedies, not only for their own sick and wounded, but the prisoners as well.

(8) That prior to the period of the greatest mortality at Andersonville, the Confederate authorities offered to release thousands of prisoners, without requiring any equivalent in exchange if the Federal Government would provide transportation for them. This offer was not accepted by the Federal Government until too late to save the lives of thousands of those who died.

(9) That the control of the prisons in the North was turned over by Secretary Stanton and the vindictive and partisan men, who were later responsible also for the crimes of Reconstruction, to the lowest element of an alien population and to negro guards of a criminal type; and that such men as President Lincoln, Seward, McClellan and the best people of the North were intentionally kept in ignorance of conditions in Northern prisons while officially furnished with stories as to "the deliberate cruelties'- practiced in the South. [9]

General Robert E. Lee, who, for a time, was held as *particeps criminis* in the alleged wholesale barbarity, but whose word has never been found to be false, says of Libby and Belle Isle: "I never knew that any cruelty was practiced, and I have no reason to believe that it was practiced. I can believe, and have reason to believe, that privations may have been experienced by the prisoners *because I know that provision and shelter could not be provided for them.*" Again he stated, in April, 1867, that "The laws of the Confederate Congress and the orders of the War Department directed that the rations furnished prisoners of war should be the same in quantity and quality as those furnished enlisted men in the army of the Confederacy, and that the hospitals for prisoners should be placed on the same footing as other ('on federate States hospitals in all respects." [10]

Turning again to Andersonville prison, we find that the official order for the location of "a Large prison" in the South in 1864 was that it should have "a healthy locality, plenty of pure water, a running stream, and, if possible, shade trees, and in the immediate neighborhood of grist and saw mills."

The Confederate authorities have been denounced because they did not cause to he constructed a sufficient number of barracks at Andersonville, since the very order for its founding required that it he in the neighborhood of saw mills. This order, was, indeed, carried out as strictly as possible in accordance with the other conditions, hut it must he remembered that the South, having very few manufactories, could not supply the tools with which to build; and that the saw mills nearest Andersonville, being very primitive affairs, were not able to supply lumber sufficient for the stockade, much less for the barracks. But few of the officers of the guard had "shanties" and these were generally built of the refuse of the mills. Some of the lumber used was brought a distance of eighty miles and all of the available rolling stock of the Confederacy was taxed to its utmost capacity in transporting supplies for the army in the field and to the prisons. Tt should also he remembered that "during the last two years of the war there was not even a tent of any description to be found in any of the armies of the Confederacy, save such as were captured from the Federals." [11]

Many writers, including the distinguished editor of "American State Trials," still refer to "The Dead Line" at Andersonville with expressions of horror, and it has been often brought forward as "prima facie evidence" that the

Southerners were intentionally barbarous and cruel, doubtless in ignorance of the fact that a "dead line" existed in Northern prisons. At Andersonville, this regulation was an absolute necessity and "consisted of stakes with a plank nailed on top and at a distance of twenty feet from the walls of the stockade." Had it not been for this precaution, less than fifteen hundred guards could never have held the thirty thousand and more prisoners under their control. This "dead line" was well defined, while in the Northern prisons it was in many cases wholly unmarked.

If there be charges of neglect and brutality in the burial of prisoners at Andersonville, the records show that the paroled prisoners were responsible to their comrades for this last duty. If there be charges as to filth in the preparation of food and cruelty in its distribution to the prisoners, it is to their paroled companions that the complaints may be carried, for they were in charge of this office. If there be charges of foul play, murder, and robbery of the helpless sick by night, the paroled prisoners may answer for it. They thereby made good their escape, and they are among those who testified that another was guilty of deeds they themselves had committed. [12]

The best known and the only specific charges of cruelty officially taken up for prosecution by the United States Government were those preferred against Captain Henry Wirz, for a while Commandant at Andersonville prison.

The charges sustained by the Military Court which declared Captain Wirz guilty, were, in brief:

"That he, the said Henry Wirz, did combine, confederate and conspire with them, the said Jefferson Davis, James A. Seddon, Howell Cobb, John II. Winder, Richard P>. Winder, Isaiah II. While, W. S. Winder, W. Shelby Reed, R. R. Stevenson, S. P. Moore, - - Kerr, Late hospital-steward at Andersonville; James Duncan, Wesley W. Turner, Benjamin Harris, and others whose names are unknown, citizens of the United States aforesaid, and who were then engaged in armed rebellion against the United States, maliciously, traitorously, and in violation of the laws of war, to impair and injure the health and to destroy the lives—by subjecting to torture and great suffering, by confining in unhealthy and unwholesome quarters, by exposing to the inclemency of winter and to the dews and burning sun of summer, by compelling the use of impure water, and by furnishing insufficient and unwholesome food—of large numbers of Federal prisoners, to wit, the number of about forty-five thousand, soldiers in the military service of the United States of America, held as prisoners of war at Andersonville, in the State of Georgia, within the line of the so-called Confederate States, on or before the 27th day of March, A. D. 1864, and at divers times between that day and the 10th day of April, A. D., 1865, to the end that the armies of the United States might be weakened and impaired, and the insurgents engaged in armed rebellion against the United States might be aided and comforted."

II. "Murder in Violation of the laws and customs of War" in certain specifications to the number of thirteen. In these "specifications," Captain Wirz is accused, while acting as Commandant, 'of feloniously, wilfully of his malice aforethought, making sundry and several assaults upon soldiers, belonging to the army of the United States, with a certain pistol, called a revolver, then and there loaded with gunpowder and bullets whereby he inflicted mortal wounds upon their bodies so that they died." Three soldiers were murdered thus, in each case the "specification" stating, "whose name is unknown." Specification No. 2 told how a soldier, name unknown, was stamped to death by said Wirz. Another prisoner was "tortured unto death in the stocks. 7 ' Several more died under specially contrived cruelties, and others were fired upon by orders from said Wirz. In each and every case, the name of the victim was "unknown."

The Military Commission declared Captain Wirz guilty of charge I and of practically all of the specifications under Charge II, and sentenced him to be hanged on the tenth day of November, 1865.

A few of the amazing circumstances connected with this trial may be given here to show that it was, perhaps, the only really infamously unjust prosecution and conviction on record in the history of the jurisprudence of the United States, unless partial exception be made as to the condemnation of Mrs. Surratt and Dr. Samuel A. Mudd, unjustly convicted of complicity in the brutal assassination of President Lincoln by the demented Booth and his ignorantly criminal accomplices.

In the first place, after ascertaining the nature and purpose of the military court appointed, in violation of the Constitution of the United States, to try Captain Wirz, the regularly employed counsel for the defense withdrew from the case. Even permission to be heard, according to law, was denied the prisoner. It may be added, by way of a sidelight on the conditions of the time, that the three men who had been brought forward by the same partisan leaders for the purpose of convicting Jefferson Davis of complicity in the assassination of President Lincoln had just been shown to be perjurers. Two had turned state's evidence against the third, Conover, who was then in jail. It was determined that no chances for a like failure were to be taken in the case of Wirz. It was, moreover, easier to convict a subaltern than a high official of the Confederacy.

Captain Wirz was placed in confinement in the Old Capitol Prison on the 7th of May, 1865; and, from that moment, the press and people of the country were fed with stories of the "monster" and "demon" Wirz. As far as possible, all favorable testimony volunteered by Federal officers and soldiers was suppressed. A victim had to be produced by radical politicians and extremists in order to keep the American people from learning (1) that the suffering in the Southern prisons could have been prevented by the Federal Government and (2) that there were at least equally terrible privations in the Northern prisons, a knowledge of which would have led their countrymen to pour out their indignation on them instead.

In the second place, Captain Wirz was accused, by the terms of Charge I, of conspiracy with Jefferson Davis and other officials of the Confederacy, in deliberately planning the death of thousands of Federal soldiers. Not a particle of evidence teas found that such a conspiracy ever existed, yet Captain Wirz was convicted of this grave charge, while his fellow "conspirators," a number of whom were actually named in the Charge, were never even brought to trial.

In the third place, the specific charges of murder brought against Captain Wirz were made by only twelve to fifteen of the one hundred and sixty former actual or alleged prisoners summoned or secured by those backing the prosecution. At least most of these, and perhaps all of them, like Conover, and his two infamous associates, were perjurers. One of the witnesses upon whose testimony Judge-Advocate Chapman laid particular stress, as being of a reliable and truthful character swore himself in as "Felix de la Baume, 1 ' a nephew of Marquis Lafayette. Upon finishing his labors on the witness stand, and before the trial was over, he was rewarded for his trouble by being appointed to a clerkship in a Department of the Federal Government, while about the same time one of the witnesses who seemed likely to offer favorable testimony for the defense, was arrested in open court, and placed behind prison bars before he could testify. Eleven days after the execution of Wirz, the alleged Monsieur de la Baume proved to be Felix Oeser of Saxony, a deserter from the 7th New York Regiment. [13]

Finally, on the day before the execution of Captain Wirz, a telegram was sent out to the effed that Wirz had made a confession which implicated Jefferson Davis. At about the same time, a message was sent to Wirz, through the medium of his minister, Father Boyle, that if he would implicate Davis, his sentence would be commuted. Furthermore, in the deliberate effort to blacken the character of Wirz and to weaken the effect of his declaration of innocence, a telegram was sent out stating on high authority that the prisoner's wife had attempted, on the 27th of October, to poison her brute of a husband, although Mrs. Wirz was, at that time, hundreds of miles away. To cap the climax, the body of the prisoner was refused a Christian burial. It is perhaps significant of ultimate justice at the bar of history, which Lincoln has truly declared "we cannot escape" that the body of Wirz was placed in the yard of the jail beside the body of Mrs. Surratt, who is now generally regarded as the innocent victim of another military commission. Surely, if Captain Wirz were "a tool" and guilty of the crimes for which he was convicted under "Charge I," the men who so infamously used him as such were far more criminal and deserving of the gallows than their underling. Why were they, too, not hanged, or at least brought to trial? The answer is given above in that those responsible for the prosecution of Wirz knew that while he, a poor subordinate officer, might be convicted in the heat of sectional passion provoked by their misrepresentations, it was quite another matter to try and to convict the great leaders of the Confederacy. They knew perfectly well that the best element—the great majority—of the Northern people would learn the truth in such a trial; and learning the truth, they would find out and punish the accusers instead of the accused.

Is it not time that the name of Major Henry Wirz be cleared of undeserved infamy, just as the names of many other innocent men have been cleared? Is it easier to let things go on as it is, so that "one man may bear the blame for all? 1 ' If so, is it right? The answer from all fair-minded Americans will be an emphatic negative.

Notes

[1] Incredible as it may seem, these quotations are taken from three of the most widely used history text-books in America at the present time. They have been written by men honored with high positions in the teaching-profession.

[2] James Ford Rhodes, for example. (Vol. V. pp. 483-515) has done better than his contemporaries in this respect; and the Photographic History of the Civil War presents an even more extended review. Elsewhere. Rhodes draws what one may call the "significantly provincial and incomplete" conclusion, (Vol. VI. p. 29, italics inserted): 'Now that the Southern people were rid of the incubus of slavery

their moral standards were the same as those at the North; and they felt that they were amenable to the public opinion of the enlightened world."

[3] This viciously false volume revives the following post-bellum slander on the officers in Forrest's command at Fort Pillow: "The rebels began an indiscriminate slaughter, sparing neither age nor sex, white nor black, soldier nor civilian. The officers and men seemed to vie with each other in the work; men, women, and even children were deliberately shot down, beaten and hacked with sabres. Some of the children, not more than ten years old, were forced to stand and face their murderers while being shot; "the sick and wounded were butchered without mercy, the rebels entering the hospital and dragging them out to be shot, or killing them as they lay unable to offer resistance. Numbers of our men were collected in lines or groups and deliberately shot; some were shot in the river; some on the bank, and the bodies of the latter, many yet living, were kicked into the Tiver. The huts and tents where the wounded had sought shelter were set on fire, both that night and the next morning, while the wounded were still in them, and those who tried to get out were shot. One man was fastened to the floor of a tent by nails through his clothing and then burned, and one was similarly nailed to the side of a building and then burned. These deeds were renewed the next morning when any wounded who still lived were sought out and shot."

[4] The historian corresponded with this Veteran's friends and acquaintances and interviewed others. One of them, a well-known and honored Judge wrote, May 7, 1917: "Shortly after the publication of his book the Grand Army of the Republic met at...and considerable feeling was expressed by ...'s comrades there. Some disagreed with him radically and the feeling against him was so intense that it prevented his election as Department Commander. He certainly would have been elected unanimously if it had not been for the publication of his book. At the time I was holding Court in .... instead of Judge...the resident Judge there, and remember talking with .... after the election. He said he regretted that his comrades took the attitude they did but nevertheless he had not stated anything but the truth in his book and if it had cost him one of his life's ambitions he could only regret the misguided attitude of his fellows, but he did not regret doing justice to a man to whom he thought grave injustice had been done." [In the above quotation, names of individuals are not given for fear of causing bitter attacks by partisans on others. All names and correspondence are on file and may be published later.]

[5] It must be remembered that this subordinate officer was convicted of conspiring with Confederate authorities in the crimes alleged to have been committed.

[6] The Confederate prisoners, including the three thousand officers confined at Johnson's Island suffered terrible tortures from both cold and hunger. Their rations were, by order of the Federal authorities, cut down to a daily portion of one-half a loaf of hard bread, and a small piece of salt pork, which was served at noon. At Fort Delaware, in the summer of 1864, the rations were reduced to two crackers, together with an inch square of pickled meat and a cup of weak coffee. The only other meal of the day consisted of two crackers with a cup of very weak bean soup. Occasionally a quarter of a loaf of light bread was substituted for the crackers. The crackers were often filled with worms, which many of the prisoners ate with a view to sustaining life. In the coldest weather two bushels of coal a day were allowed each "barracks" of 320 men. This supply of fuel lasted but a portion of the twenty-four hours. Hospital service was so bad at this prison that many of the men preferred to suffer and die among their friends in the "layers" of superimposed hard plank bunks. Official figures given out by Secretary Stanton show that 26,436 Confederates died in Northern prisons. Each man was allowed one blanket or an overcoat. Prisoners could not have both. They were deprived of money and allowed a limited amount of sutler's checks with which they could buy tobacco, etc., but no additional food. The dead, with their bodies stripped of clothing, were thrown into long ditches; so that years afterwards a Committee authorized by Congress could not determine the dead or put up tombstones.

On the other hand, it is good to record that Confederate ex-prisoners themselves, out of their poverty, erected a memorial to Colonel Richard Owen, commandant at Camp Morton, Indiana. This noble man did all he could to mitigate the hardships of prison life, and scores of Confederate prisoners confined there and transferred to other prisons have borne pathetic testimony to his allowance of both overcoats and blankets (two). The rations were limited under conditions beyond the control of Colonel Owen, but these were "mercifully changed" in order to prevent the ravages of scurvy.

[7] The point as to variety in food is very important; for the lack of a wholesome variety caused certain diseases among the prisoners not suffered by the guards and Confederate soldiers fed on the same rations. The former, for example, could not, in many cases, eat the unbolted meal to which the Southerner was accustomed. This was particularly true of the great number of German and other prisoners of foreign birth, of whom there were many thousands in the Southern prisons. The first group of prisoners sent to Andersonville were several hundred foreigners. A large number of these foreigners and many native Americans from the Northern States could not at first eat this unbolted meal without experiencing more or less serious digestive trouble which left them in a dangerously weakened condition. Towards the close of the war a trainload of Federal prisoners northward bound halted by the side of another train returning Confederate prisoners to the South. The soldiers leaned from the windows of their coaches and bantered each other. The "Yanks" hurled at the "Rebs" some pieces of the despised "corn pones" which were to be exhibited as proof of the barbarity of "Rebel" fare. To their surprise the half-starved "Rebel" prisoners seized these rejected "Rebel" rations, ate them ravenously, and yelled for more.

In 1918, under the caption, "How corn may help win the War," the United States Food Administration sent out an *advertisement which reads: "When we use more corn, the Allies—our associates in the war—can use more wheat. They can not use cornmeal instead of wheat in their daily diet, as we do, because neither their cooks nor their appetites are adapted to it."*

[8] The older partisan accounts and present comparisons based upon the accounts attempt to explain this by the statement that the Confederates refused exchange to negroes; but this point was brought up long after the cartel was systematically disregarded. There is an abundance of proof of this. The following extract from a letter from General U. S. Grant to General B. F. Butler, 18th August, 1864, over a year after the terms of the cartel were violated, is indicative of the attitude of the highest Federal officer towards exchange: "It is hard," wrote Grant, "on our men in Southern prisons not to exchange them, but it is humanity to those left in the ranks to fight our battles."

[9] This Confederate defense against the charge of wholesale and deliberate cruelty to prisoners is amply sustained by the historical evidence at hand. The impartial historian, looking for all the salient facts, does find, however, as a kind of flaw in the frankness of the Confederate statement, admissions on the part of reputable authorities that there was evidence of executive failure in the commissary department. It may be said, however, that the same failure, in a more exaggerated form., was evident in the supply department of the Army of Northern Virginia. The immediate cause of the surrender of General Lee was the failure of support on the part of his food trains.

Although it is known that Abraham, Lincoln was told of the alleged cruelties in Southern prisons and that he was urged to denounce them publicly, it is- a fact that President Lincoln never did so commit himself. There is. on the contrary, evidence to show that he did not believe them. Being a keen judge of men, he well knew the character of both the accused and the accusers, the latter including both those who wilfully misrepresented the matter and those who honestly believed the misrepresentations.

[10] *Hospital No. 21 in Richmond, Virginia, was anions those singled out for special charges of deliberate cruelty and neglect of sick prisoners. Reliable testimony by Federal officers was given (and officially suppressed) in rebuttal of these charges; but there was one incident connected with this prison hospital that is of unusual interest. At the time of the surrender of Richmond, Hospital No. 21 was under the direction of Assistant-Surgeon Alexander Tinsley. Richmond was captured on the 3rd of April. 1865: but when the Federal prisoners found that they were to lose the kind offices of this Confederate surgeon, they themselves petitioned that he be allowed to remain in charge. This was accordingly done by order of Major-General Weitzel. U. S. A. Surgeon Tinsley was later transferred with the prisoners to Jackson Hospital and remained on duty in the service of the United States Government until May 9th. or until there was no further use for his services. His modest bill of $285.00 for his own services and for fuel and board for himself and "forage" for his horse was presented to the United States Government, but it was never honored,* although the claim was brought up in the United States Senate at about the time the Hon. James G. Blaine was making his wholesale and sweeping accusations of cruelty against all the Confederate authorities in charge of the prisoners, including-Surgeon Tinsley. The Federal order appointing Dr. Tinsley had printed thereon: "Medical Director's Office, Army of the James, Before Richmond, Fa." As the writer was preparing the order, however, he triumphantly drew his pen through the long-existent "Before."

There can be no question as to the high character of Surgeon Tinsley, as well as to his unselfish devotion to duty. He testified, near the close of the war, before a Confederate Committee of investigation: "I have seen many of our prisoners returned from the North, who were nothing but skin and bones. They were as emaciated as they could be to retain life. I saw two hundred and fifty of our sick brought in on litters from the steamer at Rockett's; thirteen dead bodies were brought off the steamer that night. At least thirty died in one night after they were received."

[11] Not only were there few implements manufactured in the South for carpentering, farming, etc., but even nails were not to be had, "there being but one solitary manufactory of cut nails in the limits of the Confederacy."

[12] At the close of the war, Brigadier-General Neal Dow, U. S. V., afterwards the noted temperance reformer, and candidate for the Presidency, went to distribute clothing to the prisoners. He was greeted with profane abuse, whereupon he turned to those in charge and said, in considerable humiliation of spirit: "You have here the rakings and

scrapings of Europe." Among the brave men held prisoners at Andersonville, there was just this mercenary element to be contended with, and great numbers of fine American soldiers suffered terribly at the hands of such fellow-prisoners. The Confederacy, on the other hand, with few exceptions, could not draw upon any but its own American-born population. There was, nevertheless, an evil element among the Confederates in the Northern prisons. These were the men who took the "iron-clad oath." They were separated, in some cases, from their former comrades. They were dubbed "galvanized" prisoners, and were given more and better rations than the prisoners who remained loyal to the cause they represented.

[13] Concerning the accounts of cruelty presented in regard to the alleged "barbarous practice" of running down fugitive Federal prisoners with bloodhounds, quotations from these very witnesses are sufficient to refute the alleged fierceness of these "blood-thirsty animals." We are told by one Mr. Goss, in his scathing denunciation of the Confederate prison officials, how he, with a "rotten fence rail," held a whole pack of these ferocious hounds at bay. Another, pursued for hours by a number of these ravenous beasts, tells how. exhausted, he fell asleep only to be awakened by one of them licking his face." Still another such writer unwittingly shows us the real kindness of '"the terrible brute Wirz" by describing "the villain*' as he came into the camp on sundry occasions to warn prisoners against recklessness, lest there should be unnecessary loss of life.

As late as June, 1902, an article in the Century Magazine stated that, "Jefferson Davis. President of the Southern Confederacy, was known to have imported a pack [of bloodhounds] for breeding purposes. They were ordered destroyed. The man detailed for this work was a brother of Mr. George H. Meeker of Beatrice, Nebraska. He performed his task well, for it is said that he found and killed no fewer than forty-seven bloodhounds at Mr. Davis's home."

As a matter of fact, Mr. Davis not only did not import any bloodhounds. but he did not own any dogs at all. In the September issue of the Century Magazine the editors apologized for the error of their contributors and stated the facts, at least as far as Jefferson Davis was concerned in regard to this popular and historical misconception.

The South in the Matter of Pensions

Money for pensions has been raised by this government through a uniform system of taxation, bearing alike upon North, South, East and West. The man in the South has paid his share along with the man in the North, and his rate of taxation has all along been the same. Yet there has been a most marked difference in the amount of money received by the South through pensions as compared with the hundreds of millions paid throughout the North. While the Southern man has borne this burden cheerfully, complaining only when corruption was especially rank, it is important to note that this excess amount of pensions claimed by the North and paid to the North is not confined to pensions of the War between the States, but begins with the beginning of the pension system of this government.

The North early began to lay claim to large pensions and to receive them. From the year 1791 to the year 1833 this government paid out in pensions $29,600,000. Of this sum, approximately $20,000,000 was paid to the North, while only $9,000,000 was distributed throughout the entire South. And be it borne in mind that these pensions were paid for wars in which all fought on the same side and in which the numbers furnished by the South compare most favorably with the numbers furnished by the North. These pensions were for the Revolution and for the War of 1812, with perhaps minor wars, Indian wars, etc.

During this period there were paid out to the States severally as follows: New York, $6,186,000; Massachusetts, $3,331,000; Pennsylvania, $2,664,000; Maine, $2,115,000; Connecticut, $1,912,000; Vermont, $1,923,000; New Hampshire, $1,697,000; Virginia, $1,649,000; Kentucky, $1,192,000; and no other Southern State drew as much as one million dollars for this period from 1791 to 1833. This is a very striking comparison, and the causes for it lie in the characteristics of the people.

Now, as to pensions of the War Between the States, the South has received comparatively nothing, and yet the report of the Commissioner of Pensions iii the year L909 shows that there had been paid out up to that year the enormous sum of $3,686,000,000, and of this total the South had contributed its full share through a system of uniform taxation throughout the country.

Moreover, the South has home the burden cheerfully, making complaint only when some flagrant raid on the treasury was engineered through the Congress, such as the service pension act of February 6, 1907, where $58,000,000 per year was added to the pension burden, already loaded with fraud, and millions paid out to Northern soldiers, so called, who had never seen a battle Field nor fired a gun.

As an example of the unequal distribution of national money through pensions, take the report of the Commissioner for the year 1909, in which year $161,973,000 was disbursed. Of this sum, the eleven States which composed the Confederacy received about $12,300,000, and the North received the balance, proportioned among the States in part as follows: Ohio, $16,376,000; Pennsylvania, $15,351,000; New York, $13,912,000; Illinois, $11,311,000; Indiana, $10,640,000; and the other $80,000,000 was scattered through the remainder of Northern and New England States, with a small proportion sent abroad.

As far back as 1830 Senator Hayne, of South Carolina, complained that the pension system was being maintained as a heavy charge upon the treasury for the purpose of keeping up the system of high duties to which the South objected. He estimated that there had been distributed up to that time about $15,000,000 to the North and West and about $5,000,000 to the South. In Hayne's view the South was paying the greater portion of the money which supplied the treasury, while the public money was being expended chiefly in the North. So, even though the complaints of Northern politicians of this good year 1917 were true—and they are not—that the South, being in the saddle politically, was legislating to her exclusive advantage and receiving an unjust due of public money, the South could point to the past for her excuse and example.

Congressman Thomas U. Sisson, of Mississippi, said in a speech at Memphis in 1909: "If Mississippi received only one-fifth of the amount which Ohio receives each year for pensions, she could relieve herself of her present school tax and not pay one cent and yet run her schools eight months in the year." This further striking statement is made: "Kansas gets $5,423,000 in pensions and has a population of about 1,500,000—that is, she gets over $3.60 for every man, woman, and child in the State. If Mississippi received as much, she could run the whole State government on it each year and have over $2,500,000 left each year. What she received each year would not only run our entire State government, but would pay all the State, county, and municipal expenses. The amount paid is taken from the report for the year ending June, 1907." Congressman Sisson takes the figures from official reports of 1900 and shows how sums are paid into the following States that would equal per head for each man, woman, and child in the State the following: Ohio, over $3.50; Vermont, over $3.92; Maine, over $4; Massachusetts, $1.88.

It must be continually borne in mind that these sums are paid into these States from a fund levied upon all parts of the country alike; and while millions have thus been taken from the impoverished South and poured into the lap of the rich North, the South has paid it uncomplainingly and has at the same time taxed herself further for the support and aid of her own soldiers.

While thus from the beginning of this government the South has paid its share of taxes and borne its share of burdens, receiving only a minor portion of public disbursements, it has always measured up with great patriotism to the demands of the government, and in no way has this been exemplified more strikingly than in its subscriptions to the liberty loans. Be it remembered that every dollar subscribed to these loans by the South was subscribed from a purely patriotic motive and at a sacrifice, for in this section legal rates of interest mount to eight and ten per cent, and money can be readily invested and loaned at such rates, and the buying of a government bond paying three and a half per cent is a sacrifice; while in the wealthy North, with its great surplus of wealth and call money lending as low as one per cent, it is no sacrifice to invest in a stable government security at three and a half per cent. This is not said in criticism of the North, which is measuring up to the demands of this great war, but it illustrates that, while the South from her scantier stores patriotically furnishes what she can, she doe« it at a sacrifice not felt in the North and should receive credit therefor, even though her aggregate subscriptions may not equal the contributions of the far wealthier section.

[The above figures are obtained from Volume V., 'The South in the Building of the Nation," in chapter on "Economic Conditions," written for the series by Professor Glasson, of the Chair of Political Economy of Trinity Col-

lege, who gives as further authority "Executive Documents 2d Bess., 23d Cong., 1834-35," iii., No. 89, page 32. "The South in the Building of the Nation' 7 is published by the Southern Historical Publication Society, of Richmond, Va., with a long list of distinguished editors in chief, and the subject of "Economic History" in under the charge of Professor Ballagh, of Johns Hopkins.]

Injustice to the South

By Rev. Randolph M'Kim, D. D., LL. D., Washington, D. C.

A bishop of the Protestant Episcopal Church, speaking in Paris a year or more ago, described the Southern Confederacy as "a belligerent that was fighting to make slavery a permanent principle on which to establish and maintain national life.'" A general of the United States army, speaking to the Y. M. C. A. in New York, stated that "the issues at stake between the Allies and the Teutonic powers are the same as those that were contested between the North and South in the American Civil War—the forces of slavery and disunion on the one side and the forces of liberty and freedom on the other. An eminent British statesman in Parliament gave utterance to a similar sentiment, declaring that the struggle on which the United States has now embarked is essentially the same as that on which it embarked nearly sixty years ago in the War between the States. And a great New York daily (the Times) has proclaimed to the world that there is an essential analogy between the spirit of the Hohenzollerns and that of "the slave power with which the United States came to grips in 1861."

These utterances, in my opinion, ought not to be permitted to pass unchallenged, for they embody, first, a contradiction of the facts of history, and, second, a cruel slander against a brave and noble people. I submit that a careful and unbiased study of the history of the epoch of the American Civil War establishes beyond the power of successful contradiction that the soldiers of the Confederacy were not battling for slaves or slavery, but for the right of self-government, for the principle lately asserted by President Wilson, that "governments derive their just powers from the consent of the governed." Neither was the war inaugurated and prosecuted upon the Northern side for the purpose of liberating the slave, but for the preservation of the Union.

In support of my contention I cite, first, the testimony of Abraham Lincoln. In August, 1862, he wrote Mr. Greeley: "My paramount object in this struggle is to save the Union and is not either to save or destroy slavery. If I could save the Union without freeing any slave, I would do it; and if I could save it by freeing all the slaves, I would do it; and if I could save it by freeing some and leaving others alone, I would also do that. What I do about slavery and the colored race I do because I believe it helps to save the Union, and what I forbear I forbear because I do not believe it would help to save the Union." ("Short Life of Abraham Lincoln" by Nicolay, page 336.)

Mr. Lincoln, then, was waging the war not to free the slaves, but to save the Union, and when he issued his Emancipation Proclamation on January 1, 1863, he did not undertake to free all the slaves, but only "those persons held as slaves within any State the people whereof shall then be in rebellion against the United States." (*Idem,* page 341.)

Slaves in States not in rebellion were not released from slavery by the Emancipation Proclamation, but by the Thirteenth Amendment to the Constitution.

Moreover, Mr. Lincoln declared that the freeing of the slaves was a war measure, adopted solely because he deemed that it would further the supreme object of the war—viz., the preservation of the Union.

On the other hand, I maintain that the Southern States did not go to war for the perpetuation of slavery, but for the preservation of the principle of self-government. To say that the battle flag of the Confederacy was the emblem of slave power and that Lee and Jackson and their heroic soldiers fought not for liberty, but for the right to hold their fellow men in bondage, is to contradict the facts of history. Jefferson Davis, the President of the Confederacy, declared that the South was not fighting for slavery; and, in fact, he embarked on the enterprise of secession believing that he would as a consequence lose his slaves, for he wrote to his wife in February, 1861, "In any case our slave property will eventually be lost"—that is to say, whether successful or not in establishing the Southern Confederacy.

Lee, the foremost soldier of the South, long before the war had emancipated the few slaves that came to him by inheritance; whereas his Union antagonist, General

Grant, held on to those that had come to him through marriage with a Southern woman until they were freed by the Thirteenth Amendment. Stonewall Jackson never owned more than two negroes, a man and a woman, whom he bought at their earnest solicitation. He kept account of the wages he would have paid white labor, and when he considered himself reimbursed for the purchase money (for he was a poor man) he gave them their freedom. Gen. Joseph E. Johnston never owned a slave, nor did Gen. A. P. Hill, nor Gen. Fitzhugh Lee. Gen. J. E. B. Stuart, the great cavalry leader, owned but two, and he rid himself of both long prior to the war. (See article by Col. W. Gordon McCabe in the London *Saturday Review* of March 5, 1910.)

To this testimony of the most puissant men engaged in the conflict I add the testimony of the common soldiers of the Confederacy. With one voice then and with one voice now the Southern soldiers avowed that they were not fighting and suffering and dying for slavery, but for the right of self-government.

I was a soldier in Virginia in the campaigns of Lee and Jackson, and I declare I never met a Southern soldier who had drawn his sword to perpetuate slavery. Nor was the dissolution of the Union or the establishment of the Southern Confederacy the supreme issue in the mind of the Southern soldier. What he had chiefly at heart was the preservation of the supreme and sacred right of self-government. The men who made up the Southern armies were not fighting for their slaves when they cast all in the balance— their lives, their fortunes, and their sacred honor - and endured the hardships of the march and the camp and the perils and sufferings of the battle held. Besides, it was a very small minority of the men who fought in the Southern armies who were financially interested in the institution of slavery.

But the Southern Confederacy is reproached with the fact that it was deliberately built on slavery. Slavery, we are told, was its corner stone. But if slavery was the corner stone of the Southern Confederacy, what are we to say of the Constitution of the United States? That instrument as originally adopted by the thirteen colonies contained three sections which recognized slavery. And whereas the Constitution of the Southern Confederacy prohibited the slave trade, the Constitution of the United States prohibited the abolition of the slave trade for twenty years. And if the men of the South are reproached for denying liberty to three and one-half million of human beings at the same time that they professed to be waging a great war for their own liberty, what are we to say of the revolting colonies of 1776 who rebelled against the British crown to achieve their liberty while slavery existed in every one of the thirteen colonies unrepudiated?

Cannot these historians who deny that the South fought for liberty because they held the blacks in bondage see that upon the same principle they must impugn the sincerity of the signers of the Declaration of Independence? For while in that famous instrument they affirmed before the whole world that all men were created free and equal and that "governments derive their powers from the consent of the governed," they took no steps whatever to free the slaves which were held in every one of the thirteen colonies. No; if the corner stone of the Constitution of the Southern Confederacy was slavery, the Constitution of 1789—the Constitution of the United States—had a worse corner stone, since it held its aegis of protection over the slave trade itself. We ask the candid historian, then, to answer this question: If the colonists of 1776 were freemen fighting for liberty, though holding men in slavery in every one of the thirteen colonies, why is the tribute of loving liberty denied to the Southern men of 1861 because they too held men in bondage?

If George Washington, a slaveholder, was yet a champion of liberty, how can that title be denied to Robert E. Lee?

Slavery was not abolished in the British dominions until the year 1833. Will any man dare to say that there were no champions of human liberty in England before that time?

It will not be amiss at this point to remind your readers, especially your English readers, that the government of England and not the people of the South was originally responsible for the introduction of slavery. The colony of Virginia again and again and again protested to the British king against sending slaves to her shores, but in vain; they were forced upon her. Nearly one hundred petitions against the introduction of slavery were sent by the colonists of Virginia to the British government.

In 1760 South Carolina passed an act to prevent the further importation of slaves, but England rejected it with indignation. Let it also be remembered that Virginia was the first of all the States in the South to prohibit trade in slaves, and Georgia was the first to put such a prohibition into her organic constitution. In fact, Virginia was in advance of the whole world on this subject. She abolished the slave trade in 1778, nearly thirty years before England did and the same period before New England was willing to consent to its abolition. Again, in the convention which adopted the Federal Constitution Virginia raised her protest against the continuance of that traffic; but New England objected and, uniting her influence with that of South Carolina and Georgia, secured the continuance of the slave trade for twenty years more by constitutional provision. On the other hand, the first statute establishing slavery in America was passed by Massachusetts in December, 1641, in her code entitled "Body of Liberties." The first fugitive slave law was enacted by the same State. She made slaves of her captives in the Pequot War. Thus slavery was an inheritance which the people of the South received from the fathers; and if the States of the North after the Revolution sooner or later abolished the institution, it cannot be claimed that the abolition was dictated by moral considerations, but rather by differences of climate, soil, and industrial interests. It existed in several of the Northern States more than fifty years after the adoption of the Constitution.

I said at the outset that the utterances which I quoted from several prominent persons and from an editorial in a great American daily embodied a cruel slander against a brave and noble people. The comparison of the Southern leaders and soldiers—their motives, their aims, their methods of conducting war—with the Hohenzollern despots and their cruel officers and barbarous hordes of soldiers is truly amazing. To show its untruth and its cruel injustice it would be sufficient to quote the generous words of some of the most distinguished soldiers who fought for the Union in the sixties— such men as Gen. Francis Bartlett, Capt. Oliver Wendell Holmes, and Gen. Charles Francis Adams, of Massachusetts.

Captain Holmes, long since an eminent justice of the Supreme Court of the United States, said more than a quarter of a century ago: "We believed in the principle that the Union is indissoluble, but we equally believed that those who stood against us held just as sacred convictions that were the opposite of ours, and we respected them as every man with a heart must respect those who give all for their belief."

And Charles Francis Adams declared that "both the North and the South were right in the great struggle of the Civil War, because each believed itself right."

Mr. Rhodes, perhaps the ablest Northern historian of the war, declared that the time would come when the whole American people "will recognize in Robert K. Lee one of the finest products of American Life. As surely as the years go on we shall see that such a life can be judged by no partisan measure, but we shall come to look upon him as the English of our day regard Washington, whom a little more than a century ago they delighted to call rebel."

To compare such a pure and exalted hero as Lee with a tyrant like the Hohenzollern Emperor, or such a Christian soldier as Stonewall Jackson with a heartless commander like Hindenburg or a soulless tyrant like von Bissing, is an outrage upon the human understanding. To compare soldiers such as those who followed Joseph E. Johnston and Albert Sidney Johnston and the two Virginia commanders just named with the brutal and savage legions that have desolated Belgium and France almost passes belief. And yet the conspicuous authorities named at the outset of this article have dared to say that there is an essential analogy between the spirit of the Hohenzollerns and that of the Southern Confederacy. Let them tell us wherein consists the likeness. Did the government of the Southern Confederacy ever ruthlessly violate the freedom of any other State? Did it cherish any ambition to establish its dominion over any other part of the United States or of the world? Did it violate its plighted faith and scoff at a treaty as a "mere scrap of paper"? Is it not a fact that, with one or two exceptions, during all the four years of war the Confederate soldiers in their conduct of war respected the principles of civilization and humanity? Is it not a fact that when Lee in his offensive-defensive campaign of 1863 invaded the State of Pennsylvania his soldiers not only were not guilty of any barbarity or of any rapine, but so respected private property that in the three weeks they were marching and fighting on the soil of Pennsylvania they left behind them not a single print of the iron hoof of war? And yet men of God and officers high in rank and editors of commanding ability have not hesitated to institute a comparison between the Hohenzollerns and what they are pleased to call the slave power of the South. Let me say to them that if they would find a parallel to the spirit of the Hohenzollerns as that spirit has been displayed in this tremendous war against liberty, they will find it in the record of the pillage and rapine and the desolation inflicted by the soldiers of the Union and their camp followers in the Shenandoah Valley of Virginia under Sheridan's orders and in the States of South Carolina and Georgia under the orders of General Sherman.

Here is what Gen. Charles Francis Adams says on that subject: "Sherman's advancing army was enveloped and followed by a cloud of irresponsible stragglers * * * known as bummers, who were simply for the time being desperadoes bent on pillage and destruction, subject to no discipline, amenable to no law; * * * in reality a band of Goths. Their existence was a disgrace to the cause they professed to serve."

General Adams continues: "Our own methods during the final stages of the conflict were sufficiently described by General Sheridan when, during the Franco-Prussian

War, as the guest of Bismarck, he declared against humanity in warfare, contending that the correct policy was to treat a hostile population with the utmost rigor, leaving them, as he expressed it, 'nothing but their eyes to keep with.' In other words, a veteran of our civil strife, General Sheridan, advocated in an enemy's country the sixteenth-century practices of Tilly, described by Schiller, and the later devastation of the Palatinate, commemorated by Goethe." ("Military Studies," pages 266, 267.)

Note also that these acts of plunder and cruelty were not practiced by the bummers only, but by officers and soldiers. I have recently read again the description of an eyewitness, that learned and accomplished man, Dr. John Bachman, of South Carolina, honored with membership in various societies in England, France, Germany, Russia, etc., and the narrative reads like a description of the devastation and cruelty and barbarian practices of the soldiers of Van Kluck in Belgium and France. One sentence may suffice here: "A system of torture was practiced toward the weak, unarmed, and defenseless which, so far as I know and believe, was universal throughout the whole course of that invading army." Not only aged men but delicate women were made the subjects of their terrorism. Even the blacks were "tied up and cruelly beaten." Several poor creatures died under the infliction.

There, and not in the armies of the South, will be found a parallel to the spirit of the Hohenzollerns.

The Secession of 1861 Founded Upon Legal Right

By E. W. R. Ewing, A. M., LL. B., LL. D., Historian-in-Chief, S. C. V.
Author of "Legal and Historical Status of the Dred Scott Decision." &c.

Secession rested upon fundamental law. The secession from the United States by the several States of the South in 1861, which led to the war between the Confederacy and the Federal Government aided by the remaining States, was within constitutional right found in that greatest governmental instrument, the Constitution of the United States. That secession was the extreme means, in the sense that the right of revolution as such a means is sometimes jus-titled, for the purpose of preserving the sacredness and blessings of written constitutional government, *and for these purposes only.*

Now brush the cobwebs and preconceived notions from the mental vision and let us measure by the sternest logic and the strictest of universally recognized rules these sweeping premises, standards of conduct for which our fathers fought and for which many gave their lives and for which our mothers made the most supreme sacrifices.

First, then exactly what do we mean by secession? We are to examine specific conduct, not the mere academic definition of the word secession. The question before us is: What is meant by the secession of certain States in the southern part of the United States in 1861?

For the purpose of finding the legal ground upon which those Southern States acted, it is immaterial whether we regard the acts comprehended by the word secession in this connection as accomplished or attempted secession, but it is interesting to recall that those in the exercise of the chief functions of the Federal Government and a large part of Northern people generally insisted in 1861 (contrary to prior Northern doctrine and practice) that no Southern State could secede, could get out of the Union; while four years later, after the South had worn out her swords and had broken her bayonets, and her brave boys were mostly asleep beneath the golden rods of the summer and the withering leaves of somber winter, the same pro-Union people generally and the functionaries of the United States Government were sordid and cruel in holding that the seceding States were out of the Union and as sovereign and independent States had ceased to functionate as units of the Union! So to avoid confusion of thought upon this point it may be assumed without fear of successful contradiction that the seceding States were at least *de facto* out of the Union.

That a course of conduct does not reach its final goal is no evidence that it was not legally taken. So the secession here under consideration may be broadly and correctly defined as the act or acts of the Southern State's, each exercising what we call its sovereign political powers, the purpose of which was to sever allegiance to and connection with the Union.

The Union was and yet is the relation between each State and a sovereignty known as the United States (or the Federal Government) which was created by and which exists by the authority of that wonderful, written instrument known as the Constitution of the United States.

Hence secession was the act of a State as such by which it at least sought to become and for a time was de facto independent of the United States, out of the Union, just as each colony became by revolution independent of and out of the British Empire back in 1776.

Mr. Lincoln who was at the time as President the chief executive of the United States took the position that no State could withdraw and become completely independent. So as the Southern States one by one persisted in the secession course Mr. Lincoln sent Federal troops into the South to re-establish where broken and to maintain Federal authority—not to free the slaves or affect in the least slavery. To resist this invasion by armed force the seceding States raised troops to defend the newly asserted independence, just as the colonies did back in 1776 with regard to Great Britain, the Southern States organizing in the meantime a central government known as the Confederate States of America. Thus the war came on apace.

Then since secession was either a withdrawal or an effort to withdraw from the Union, to become completely independent of the government of the United States, our first inquiry must be: What is the relation of each state to the Union? In finding this relation we necessarily define the government of the United States, also called the Federal Government.

The first thing we discover, as just intimated, when we come to see exactly what the American Union is, when we really discern the universally acknowledged fundamental of all fundamentals regarding its existence, is that the Constitution is the one source of its power and authority, the sole source of its vitality; and so outside of or minus this Constitution there would be no Union, no United States of America. This great, basal truth is one of the settled and established facts concerning our American government.

In 1816, when Marshall of Virginia and Story of Massachusetts, two great constitutional lawyers, were members of the bench, the Supreme Court of the United State, the entire bench concurring said:

"The government, then, of the United States can claim no powers which are not granted to it by the Constitution, and the powers actually granted must be such as are expressly given, or given by accessary implication." (1 Wheaton (U. S. Reports), 326.)

In 1906 Mr. Justice Brewer, speaking Tor that same high court, said: "As heretofore stated the constant declaration of this court from the beginning is that this government (of the United States) is one of enumerated powers."

Then as showing the place where that enumeration is found the court in 1906 quoted with entire approval the words from the decision, as written by Story of Massachusetts in 1816, "the United States can claim no powers which are not granted to it by the Constitution."

This fact, a most basal truth, is found not alone in the decisions of the courts; but it is the great principle by which all departments of the Federal Government are admittedly controlled. Tt is the practical fact in all the activities of the general government.

There is another similarly fundamental truth, practical fact:

The United States government does not enjoy spontaneous or original or inherent sovereignty; all of its sovereign powers are *delegated.* This fact is just as universally and as practically recognized as the other. "The government of the United States is one of *delegated,* limited, and enumerated powers," is one of the hundreds of statements of this truth repeated by the Supreme Court in case of the United States vs. Harris (106 U. S. (Supreme Court Reports), 635.).

There is a dispute whether the States created the Federal Government, *delegated* to it the powers it has, or whether it is the creature of the whole people of the

United States acting as a great sovereign political unit. It appears to me, since the Constitution went from its framers back to the States, *back to each separate State for its independent action,* too clear for argument that it is the creature of the States, particularly since three-fourths of the States had to approve it before it became operative and three-fourths may now amend it. (Constitution, Art. V.).

And all the more that this must be true when we recall that at the formation of the Federal Government and before the ratification of the Constitution, "thirteen dependent colonies became thirteen independent States;" that is, in other words, before the ratification of the Constitution "each State had a right to govern itself by his own authority and its own laws, without any control by any other power on earth." (Ware vs. Hilton, 3 Dallas, 199; McIlvaine vs. Coxe, 4 Cranch, 212; Manchester vs. Mass., 139 U. S. 257; Johnson vs. McIntosh, 8 Wheaton, 395; Shivley vs. Bowlby, 152 U. S. 14.) But we need not stop to debate this question here or let it bother us in considering secession. At the time of secession we had a certain kind of government, the same we have now, in fact; and however it was created we know that the universally admitted facts are that the Federal Government gets its vital breath from the Constitution; that all its powers are *enumerated* in that Constitution and are *delegated through it.*

Regardless of from whom or from what delegated, this fact of the delegation from *some other completely sover-*

eign power is an important one in considering secession. Many errors have been made by confusing the powers of the United States as they might be under the general nature of sovereignty with what they really are under the limited and delegated sovereignty it really has. "The government of the United States has no inherent common law prerogative and it has no power to interfere in the personal or social relations of citizens by virtue of authority deducible from the general nature of sovereignty," as a recognized law authority correctly states the actual practical and accepted fact. (39 Cyc. 694).

Then, the United States being a government of limited powers, lacking any power over very many subjects which must be controlled or produce chaotic confusion, it follows that the powers or sovereignty wherein the United States is limited, which were never entrusted to it, must rest somewhere. As summarized by a leading law authority, deduced from universally admitted decisions, here is full government in America:

"The powers of sovereignty in the United States are divided between the government of the Union and those of the States. They are each sovereign with respect to the objects committed to it, and neither sovereign with respect to the objects committed to the other." (26 Ruling Case Law, 1417.)

Here is the same truth in the language of the justices of the supreme court of Massachusetts:

"It was a bold, wise and successful attempt to place the people under two distinct governments, each sovereign and independent within its own sphere of action, and dividing the jurisdiction between them, not by territorial limits, and not by the relation of superior and subordinate, but by classifying the subjects of government and designating those over which each has entire and independent jurisdiction." (14 Gray (Mass. Reports), 616.)

In 1904 the Supreme Court of the United States stated the same fact in these words:

"In this republic there is a dual system of government, National and State, and each within its own domain is supreme." (Matter of Heff, 197 U. S. 505.)

In an opinion written for the court by Mr. Justice Day of Ohio, the same high court in 1917 said:

"The maintenance of the authority of the States over matters purely local is as essential to the preservation of our institutions as is the conservation of the supremacy of the Federal power in all matters entrusted to the Nation by the Federal Constitution.

"In interpreting the Constitution, it must never be forgotten that the Nation is made up of States to which are entrusted the powers of local government. And to them and to the people the powers not expressly delegated to the National Government arc reserved. The power of the States to regulate their purely internal affairs by such laws as seem wise to the local authority is inherent and has never been surrendered to the general government." (Hammer v. Dagenhart, 247 IT. S. 275.)

Then, it is clear and certain, the Union is one of States—States each of which is as absolutely and independently sovereign with reference to the objects or affairs not committed to the government of the United States as is the United States with reference to the specific, delegated and enumerated objects and affairs within its jurisdiction solely by virtue of the Constitution. And don't forget the distinction: the sovereignty of the United States is delegated; that of each State is *inherent.* Hence, some light upon the sovereignty of the State may rightly be had from a consideration of the nature of sovereignty in general.

These all-important facts were well understood and recognized by the seceding States in 1861. The war of 1861 to 1865 did not change the nature of our government or abate in the least the dignity of the inherent sovereignty of each State. Over and again the Supreme Court of the United States finds it necessary to emphasize this truth. Many persons are under the erroneous impression that in any and all case of unreconcilable conflict between the United States and a State over any and all subjects the decision and action of the United States becomes the supreme law of the land. Nay, not so, as the above evidence proves to any open mind. And I earnestly desire that particularly our young men and women of the South will bear this governmental fact in mind when considering the secession by Southern States in 1861. And this, too, by all means:

Each State has a most vital attribute the United States has not under the law of the Constitution. Without the States or in case of an ignored or otherwise abrogated

Constitution, the United States as a government, *the Union, ceases to exist.* On the other hand, in the words of the Supreme Court in 1868 when there certainly were no pro-secessionists on the bench:

"The people of each State compose a State, having its own government and endowed with all the functions essential to separate and independent existence." (Lane County v. Oregon, 7 Wallace, 71; Texas v. White, Id. 725; Pollock v. Farmers' &c, 157 U. S. 560; X. B. Co. v. U. S., 193 U. S. 348.)

There you are! Don't stop to quarrel as to who or what created this situation, this peculiar and dual government, this distinctively American government These definitions and illustrations state it as it was as soon as the Constitution superseded the Articles of Confederation, as it was at secession, as it is. The results of the war for the independence of the Confederacy somewhat dulled the usual conception of the reality, of the dignity, of the real nature of State sovereignty; and my earnest hope is that we shall from now on swing back to the true grasp of what the American States each is, to that universal understanding which the States had when the Constitution was adopted, for, after all, again it must be remembered, that greatest instrument is construed in the light of the contemporaneous history and existing conditions at its formation and adoption. "That which it meant when adopted it means now," said the Supreme Court in Scott v. Sandford, 19 Howard, 426, a rule followed universally.

(See, among many, Missouri v. Illinois, 180 XL S. 219; In re Debts, 158 IT. S. 591; S. C. V. U. S., 199 U. S. 450.)

Now, aside from its practical bearing upon the problems which arise today and those which will press for solution tomorrow, here is the bearing of all this upon the historical interpretation of secession : If the delegated powers of the Federal Government are perverted by those exercising them, or misused or non-used, or powers not granted are assumed, persistently, endangering the domestic peace of a State, and this condition is backed and encouraged by a great bulk of opinion in other States and aided and abetted by laws of those other States, *what is to be done by the suffering State?* What would have been the answer to this question by *any State*, North or South, at the formation of the United States?

Meet the issue squarely. Grant that such a condition has arisen, where are we? Such a condition existing, there remain the sovereign powers of the State, *the admittedly undelegated and inherent sovereignty*, having all the machinery of local government *adequate when not thus obstructed* for the protection of the domestic peace, for the defense of the property and lives of its citizens, "endowed with all the functions essential to separate and independent existence," and thus equipped, thus endowed, mind you, under and pursuant to the Constitution, *according to the fundamental law.* Fundamental law because constitutionally recognized and guaranteed, notwithstanding the inherent and reserved powers of each State are not derived from the Constitution. In the light of the contemporaneous history and existing conditions, to this question what would have been the answer of the people of any State when they insisted at ratification upon and obtained the Tenth Amendment:

"The powers not delegated to the United States by the Constitution, nor prohibited by it to the States, are reserved to the States respectively, or to the people."

The answer must be that each State would have said that thus guarded the Constitution left to it, *in the event of the conditions which I have assumed,* the right to defend the admitted inherent sovereignty by any means adequate for that purpose. "The Constitution is a written instrument. As such its meaning does not alter. That which it meant when adopted it means now." "The Constitution is to be interpreted by what was the condition of the parties to it when it was formed, by their objects and purposes in forming it, and by the actual recognition in it of the dissimilar institutions of the States."

There is another Fundamental rule followed in the interpretation of the Constitution, and that is that light is found in declarations by the States when ratifying that instrument, in Imparting to the United States the breath of Life which it would never have had but for the action of three-fourths of the States concerned. So also we go to the debates of the ratifying conventions and "to the views of those who adopted the Constitution" and get all the light possible from contemporaneous history and existing conditions. (For leading authorities see 4 Ency. U.

S. Court Reports, pages 36 and 11.) One great mistake too many make in examining the legal justification of secession is to see it too exclusively in the light of today and under the brighter conditions subsequent to that war. Such an error is fatal to a just estimate of secession. The question is: Did the States think they were getting into "an entangling alliance" from which, come whatever woe might befall, they could not withdraw? Do the light from ratifying conventions, the views of those who ratified the Constitution, and the weight of contemporary history indicate that the States meant forever to surrender for whatever domestic evil might result some of their most important attributes of sovereignty? I don't see how any open minded and sincere mind can in the light of the great bulk of the evidence upon these questions relating to the formation and vitalization of the United States believe that under any interpretation of the Constitution that instrument was meant to take from the States or from a State forever the invaluable right of resuming the delegated sovereignty when in the wisdom of the people of a State such a resumption (that is, secession) appeared necessary for domestic peace and to protect and make effective the undelegated sovereignty. Mr. Justice Catron, of the Supreme Court of the United States, quoting from the famous *Federalist* "in favor of State power," said:

"These remarks were made to quiet the fears of the people, and to clear up doubts on the meaning of the

Constitution then before them for adoption by the State conventions." (License Cases, 5 Howard, 607.)

The great bulk of the people of the several then totally independent States were afraid of the centralized power about to be loaned to the United States Government; and the right to resume the delegated powers should the experiment become unhappy was the great reason which brought the States to embark upon the venture. They were sure they had fixed the fundamental documents so that they might legally, constitutionally and morally rightly get out if any State so desired. Some of the ratifying conventions sought to make assurance doubly sure, Virginia, for instance, interpreting the Constitution as part of her ratification, said:

"The powers granted under the Constitution * * * may be resumed by the people" "whensoever the same shall be perverted to their injury or oppression."

New York followed by Rhode Island, as part of the *res gestae*, with reference to the powers delegated to the Federal Government, said that "the powers of government may be resumed by the people whenever it shall become necessary to their happiness."

Applying with such evidence a proper reasoning deducible from the general nature of sovereignty, it follows that the existence of a sovereignty "endowed with all the functions essential to separate and independent existence" must have the attribute of self-defense. The right of self-defense implies the right to choose the method. That is not sovereignty which has not the right of self-preservation. Sovereignty without the right of self-determined existence is unthinkable. Sovereignty must be dignified by all that the word implies. "As men whose intentions require no concealment generally employ the words which most directly and aptly express the ideas they intend to convey, the enlightened patriots who framed our Constitution, and the people who adopted it, must be understood to have intended what they have said," correctly said Chief Justice Marshall in Gibbons v. Ogden (9 Wheaton, 188. See also Kidd v. Pearson, 128 U. S. 20; McPherson v. Blacker, 146 U. S. 36; Hodges v. U. S. 203 U. S., 16.) There can be no such thing as limited sovereignty. There is division of sovereign powers; and that is the condition under and by virtue of the Constitution in this country. But sovereignty is a self-explanatory word and meant at secession exactly what it meant at the adoption of the Constitution.

Shortly before leaving the bench in 1915 Mr. Justice Hughes of New York prepared the opinion in Kennedy v. Becker (241 U. S. 563). As thus prepared this opinion was subsequently adopted and delivered by Chief Justice White as the unanimous opinion of the Supreme Court. Concerning the power of the State of New York to control lands which were the subject of a treaty between Robert Morris and the Seneca Nation of Indians in 1797, the court says:

"But the existence of the sovereignty of the State was well understood, and this conception involved all that was necessarily implied in that sovereignty, whether fully appreciated or not."

Upon that impregnable position stood each seceding State in 1861.

In the South we are coming too much to whisper that; "our fathers did their duty as they saw it." We should be calling to the world from the housetop that our Confederate fathers were right. For historical truth we should speak in no uncertain terms in the schools, should sound the facts in trump-blasts wherever the subject is under consideration; we should let the world know that we know that those fathers are entitled to as much glory for their defense of their wives, their mothers, their children, the domestic peace of their State by wielding the inherent sovereignty to recall the delegated and misused sovereignty, as in the defence of that delegated sovereignty against a European foe, a defence which the South rendered gladly in our war with Spain [1] and which she rendered so brilliantly in our war with Germany that the right of local self-government might Dot perish from the earth! "To insure domestic tranquillity"—one of the five reasons assigned in the preamble as the grounds for the establishment of the Constitution of the United States—to better safeguard the lives of the women and children of the South; to avert a destruction of some of the State's most important inherent powers of sovereignty,—in short, to escape imminent disaster involving the most vital and basal human rights, the seceding States faced one or two courses of action, short of the most servile submission to the greatest wrongs: they must either withdraw from the Union ; or, remaining in the Union resort to armed force against Northern States and the Federal Government. But the situation at that day can best be appreciated when we consider the constitutional facts here briefly outlined in the immediate light of what constituted the imminent disaster, the ominous peril which shrouded the South in increasing gloom. There is not space here, unfortunately, to discuss those powerful causes of that secession. [2] Those causes are too inadequately presented in text-books and too little taught even in the South. The production of this work, however, by the Sons of Confederate Veterans is one among other happy signs of a revival in the interest of historical truth. The truth and the whole truth, is the battle cry of the great organization of which I have the honor to be Historian-in-Chief,—a cry uttered from the soul of sincerity and without the least thought or purpose of animosity or bitterness. In the interest of history, for we do teach the children something about the great war which followed secession, and to be just to our Confederate fathers we must have a fuller grasp of the fundamental legal grounds of secession and of the weighty causes which moved the South—not that she believed in secession at will but solely and as an extreme measure—to resume certainly *de facto* the sovereignty delegated to the United States.

When the causes of secession are considered in the light of constitutional fundamentals herein outlined, we more readily avoid the illogical contention sometimes met which insists "that the results of the war settled the question against the secessionists." Well, well!! It is axiomatic that war settles no great question! Didn't the better thinking part of the world gladly agree to reverse the decision of a great question Germany thought she had settled forever by a decisive war? And didn't that reversal of the work of gory, cruel brute force restore to wronged and outraged France suffering Alsace-Loraine? Ah, and more: America justly poured out her blood and lavished her gold in that great world war just closing to help establish for the benefit of all people the principles upon which rest our separation from Great Britain and the *de facto* secession of the Southern States: the inalienable right of a people to break away from an objectionable and hurtful government!

There will never be another Southern secession. Nobody thinks of it as a remedy for anything now; and no part of this Union will ever *dare repeat the Northern nullification* of the Constitution to avoid the evils of which—and not to destroy the Union and not to protect or to perpetuate negro slavery—secession became the remedy to preserve the sacred binding power of a written Constitution without which the Union perishes certainly; and again because the Federal Government will never again be as limp and spineless and complacent in defending the South against such evils as nullification and other wrongs by Northern States and some Northern people, to escape all of which our fathers found secession the one probably bloodless remedy, justified by fundamental constitutional law, and the one available remedy with honor.

Notes

[1] Major Ewing, the author of this chapter, volunteered to defend the United States in that war and rendered ardent service to the United States in the war with Germany.—Editorial note.

[2] The author of this chapter hopes to reprint in booklet this contribution together with a brief presentation of the causes of secession. For particulars write Cobden Publishing Company, Ballston, Virginia.

The South and Germany

By Lyon G. Tyler, President of William and Mary College, Va.

At the moment when the United States had declared war against Germany, there seemed to be a concerted effort by Northern speakers and writers to east slurs upon the old South by drawing analogies between it and Germany. This course was taken without any regard for the feelings of the present generation of Southern men, who see no reason to be ashamed of the conduct of their ancestors.

Probably the most vicious of these attacks appeared in the *New York Times*. Under the title of "The Hohenzollerns and the Slave Power," the spirit of the old South to 1861 is said to have been essentially analogous to that of Germany. The slave power was "arbitrary, aggressive, oppressive." "The slave power proclaimed the war which was immediately begun to be a war of defence in the true Hohenzollern temper." "The South fought to maintain and extend slavery, and slavery was destroyed to the great and lasting gain of the people who fought for it, so that within a score of years from its downfall, the Southern people would not have restored it had it been possible to do so."

Here is the old trick of representing the weaker power the aggressive factor in history. An earlier instance of it occurs in the history of the Times's own State. The early New England writers in excusing their own aggressiveness represent the rich New T England colonies with their thousands as in imminent danger of being wiped out and extinguished by the handful of Dutchmen at New York. And so it has been with the Southern question. In one breath the Northern historian has talked like the Times of the "arbitrary, aggressive and oppressive power" of the South, and in the next has exploited figures to show the declining power of the South from the Revolution down to 1861. With its "indefensible institution" the South's attitude w r as necessarily a purely defensive one, and Calhoun never at furthest asked any more than a balance of power to protect its social and economic fabric. The North began the attack in 1785 with a proposition to cede to Spain the free navigation of the Mississippi River. In 1820, it attacked again when Missouri applied for admission as a State with a constitution which permitted slavery. It attacked once more in 1828 and 1832, when, despite the earnest protest of the South, it fastened on the country the protective tariff system; and the attack was continued till both Congress and the presidency w r ere controlled by them. When in pursuance of the decision of the Supreme Court the Southerners asked for the privilege of temporarily holding slaves in the Western territories until the population was numerous enough in each territory to decide the continuance of slavery for itself, it was denied them by the North. It is certain that if nature had been left to regulate the subject of slavery, not one of the Western territories would have had slavery—the odds, by reason of emigration and unfitness of soil and climate, being so greatly against it.

Did the slave power "proclaim the war" as the *Times* asserts? Every sensible man knows that the South would have been very glad to have had independence without war. But Lincoln made the ostensible ground of the war an attack on Fort Sumter, when after vacillating for almost a month, he forced the attack, contrary to the advice of his own cabinet, by sending an armed squadron to reinforce the Fort. Not a man was killed, and yet Lincoln without calling Congress, which had the sole power under the constitution, suspended the writ of habeas corpus, instituted a blockade, and set to work to raise and organize an army to subdue the South. President Wilson waited for two years till two hundred American citizens had been killed by the Germans, and even then took no hostile step without the action of Congress. Who had the "Hohenzollern temper"—the North or the South in 1861?

Did the "South fight to maintain and extend slavery?" The South fought for independence and the control of its own actions, but it did not fight to extend slavery. So far from doing this, by secession the South restricted slavery by handing over to the North the Western territory, and its constitution provided against the importation of slaves from abroad.

Slavery was indeed destroyed by the war, and it is perfectly true that no one in the South would care to restore it. At the same time we see no reason why we should be grateful for the way in which slavery was destroyed. At the beginning of the Union, there was a strong sentiment in the Southern States, especially in Maryland, Virginia and North Carolina, against the existence of slavery, but the action of three of the New England States in joining with the two extreme Southern States to keep open the slave trade for twenty years through an article in the constitution, and the subsequent activity of New England shipping in bringing thousands of negroes into the South, made its abolition a great difficulty.

No country ever waged a war on principles more different from Germany than did the Southern States. Germany justified its campaigns of "frightfulness" on the plea of necessity, but in any result its national entity was secure. The South, on the other hand, knew that failure in arms would mean the extinction of its national being, but there were some things it could not do even to preserve this, and so Robert E. Lee commanded her armies on land and Raphael Semmes roved the sea, but no drop of innocent blood stained the splendor of their achievements.

While I am glad to say that the North did not go as far as Germany the general policy of its warfare was the same —one of destruction and spoliation, and the campaigns of Sheridan and Sherman will always stand in history in the catalogue of the cruel and inhumane.

The expulsion of the inhabitants of Atlanta and the burning of the city was the prototype of the martyrdom of Louvain. Rheims and its ancient cathedral have suffered less from the shells of the Germans than beautiful Columbia and Savannah suffered from the torch and wanton depredation of the Federal soldiers.

In an article in a prominent magazine a writer quotes Lincoln's Gettysburg address and states that these last words of his speech— "That the nation shall under God have a new birth of freedom, and that government of the people, by the people, for the people shall not perish from the earth." described the great cause for which Lincoln sent armies into the field. Here is the same lack of logic and historic accuracy. The North had been antagonistic to the South from the first days of union, but it was really the jealousy of a rival nation. The chief elements that first entered into the situation were antagonistic interests and different occupations. Manufacturers were arrayed against agriculture, a protective tariff against tariff for revenue. Long before the quickening of the Northern conscience, and while the slave trade was being actively prosecuted by men from New England, that section was particularly violent against the South. Its dislike of the great democrat Jefferson went beyond all words, and he was described by the Chief Justice of Massachusetts as "an apostle of atheism and anarchy, bloodshed and plunder" How much of real opposition to slavery was mixed with this old-time jealousy in the Republican plank against slavery in the territories in 1860 no one can exactly say. But with the exception of the abolitionists, all persons—Democrats and Republicans alike—were unanimous in saying that there was no intention of interfering with slavery in the States. Lincoln was emphatically of this view, and so declared in his inaugural address.

In instituting hostilities soon after, had he avowed that he wished to raise armies to fight the South for a "new birth of freedom" and to keep popular government "from perishing from the earth," he would have been laughed at. Had he avowed his purpose of raising armies for the abolition of slavery, none but the abolitionists would have joined him. He obtained his armies only by repeatedly declaring that he waged war merely for preserving the Union.

Officers

Sons of Confederate Veterans 1919-1920

Commander-in-Chief, N. B. Forrest, Biloxi, Miss.
Adjutant-in-Chief, Carl Hinton, Denver, Colo.

Staff

Quartermaster-in-Chief, Jno. Ashley Jones, Atlanta, Ga.
Inspector-in-Chief, K. Henry Lake, Memphis, Tenn.
Commissary-in-Chief, Chas. P. Rowland, Savannah, Ga.
Judge Advocate-in-Chief, A. L. Gaston, Chester, S. C.
Surgeon-in-Chief, Dr. W. C. Galloway, Wilmington, N. C.
Chaplain-in-Chief, Rev. Henry W. Battle, Charlottesville, Va.
Historian-in-Chief, E. W. E. Ewing, Washington, D. C.

Executive Council

N. B. Forrest, Biloxi, Miss., Ex-Officio Chairman.
Edgar Scurry, Wichita Falls, Tex.
W. McDonald Lee, Irvington, Va.
J. W. McWilliams, Monroe, La.
J. Roy Price, Washington, D. C.
Carl Hinton, Denver, Colo.

Advisory Committee

Clarence J. Owens, Washington, D. C,
Chairman. Ernest G. Baldwin, Roanoke, Va.
Seymour Stewart, St. Louis, Mo.
W. W. Old, Jr., Norfolk, Va.
W. N. Brandon, Little Rock, Ark.
E. B. Haughton, St. Louis, Mo.
J. W. Apperson, Biloxi, Miss.
Carl Hinton, Denver, Colo.

Department Commanders

Army No. Va. Dept., Jas. F. Tatem, Norfolk, Va.
Army Tenn. Dept., B. A. Lincoln, Columbus, Miss.
Army Trans.-Miss. Dept., S. H. King, Jr., Tulsa, Olda.

Division Commanders

Alabama, Dr. W. E. Quin, Fort Payne.
Arkansas, A. D. Pope, Magnolia.
Colorado, H. W. Lowrie,
Denver. Dist. Columbia, A. S. Parry, Washington, D. C.
Florida, S. L. Lowry, Tampa.
Georgia, Walter P. Andrews, Atlanta.
Kentucky, E. E. Johnston, Mayfield.
Louisiana, J. W. McWilliams, Monroe.
Maryland, Henry Hollyday, Jr., Easton.
Mississippi, D. M. Featherston, Holly Springs.

Missouri, Todd M. George, Independence.
North Carolina, Geo. M. Coble, Greensboro.
Oklahoma, Tate Brady, Tulsa.
South Carolina, Weller Rothrock, Aiken.
Tennessee, D. S. Etheridge, Chattanooga.
Texas, C. A. Wright, Fort Worth.
West Virginia, Ralph Darden, Elkins.
Virginia, S. L. Adams, South Boston.
South West, E. P. Bujac, Carlsbad, N. M.

Made in the USA
Middletown, DE
15 June 2021